The public realm and the public self

The political theory of Hannah Arendt

SHIRAZ DOSSA

Wilfrid Laurier University Press

Canadian Cataloguing in Publication Data

Dossa, Shiraz
 The public realm and the public self

Bibliography: p.
Includes index.
ISBN 0-88920-967-7

1. Arendt, Hannah.   2. Political science —
Philosophy.   I. Title.

JC251.A74D68   1989   320.5'3'0924   C88-094398-X

Copyright © 1989

WILFRID LAURIER UNIVERSITY PRESS
Waterloo, Ontario, Canada   N2L 3C5

89 90 91 92 4 3 2 1

Cover design by Rachelle Longtin

Printed in Canada

FOR MY PARENTS

About the author

SHIRAZ DOSSA teaches political theory and political development at St. Francis Xavier University in Nova Scotia. He is the author of a number of essays and reviews which have been published in the *Review of Politics*, *Philosophy and Social Criticism*, *Canadian Journal of Political Science*, *Alternatives*, *Arab Studies Quarterly* and *MERIP*. In the academic years 1985-87, he held the University of Calgary University Research Fellowship in political theory and comparative politics (developing nations). He received his Ph.D. from the University of Toronto.

Contents

Preface

WE DO NOT SAY that a man who takes no interest in politics is a man who minds his own business; we say that he has no business here at all.

This, then, is the kind of city for which these men, who could not bear the thought of losing her, nobly fought and nobly died.

Thucydides*

These are some of the fine words spoken by Pericles in the course of his funeral oration. The city is Athens, the occasion is the death of those who died in its defence, and the purpose, to praise the noble city and its noble citizens in their hour of grief and glory. Pericles' words make it plain that the main business and the greatness of Athens has to do with public affairs: with the affairs common to all. His words deftly essay a manner of life at once arduous and full of risk yet filled with the joys of friendship and common striving towards excellence. But above all Pericles lauds the citizen, the *zoon politikon*, as the heart and the soul of the city. This is the city of courageous and fair public men, the city of men who prefer community and public conversation, to privacy, wealth and meretricious gossip.

Athens as Pericles describes it is both fact and fiction. Athenian practice is the source of his remarks but the essence of his praiseworthy picture is provided by his imagination nurtured on the grand poetry of Homer. Pericles paints Athens and Athenians in the heroic mould of Homer. He exaggerates rather than distorts, embellishes rather than plainly states the greatness of Athens and its way of life. His words are spoken at the beginning of the end: they seek to present to posterity Athens and its citizens at their best.

Periclean Athens and its celebration of the public life of the *polis* — its democratic temper, the virile virtuosity of its citizens, its keen passion for competitive excellence — is the powerful image at the heart of Hannah Arendt's political theory. In all facets and in almost all of her writings, this

---

* *History of the Peloponnesian War* (Harmondsworth: 1972), 147-148.

image of the Athenian *polis* and the greatness of its ways appears again and again. For her it is not an aesthetic ideal to be admired for its own sake, although that element is certainly present. Her evident purpose is to critically resurrect the Periclean ideal of citizenship as an intrinsically worthy part of human life and worthy of imitation by modern men. Thus she devotes a substantial part of her theoretical effort to unravelling the fastidious character of politics within the context of the human condition.

For Arendt politics, in its classically ancient sense, takes in a large chunk of the life men share together and it endows that life with peculiar human meaning. Politics is a particular and meaningful manner of living together; properly understood it is rewarding as well as practical. Without politics men will survive but that is all they will do. In the absence of politics individual and social life will be poor in moral wealth and human excellence. This is in part what lies hidden in the glory that was once Athens. Hidden because both the tradition of political theory and the modern age, in the main, attach hardly any significance to the shared life of citizenship, to the Athenian ideal of politics.

From Plato to Marx, Machiavelli and young Marx the decisive exceptions, the tradition of political theory either ignores or argues against the ideals of ancient citizenship. *Vita activa* and particularly the greatness of political action do not receive their due meed in the tradition. This is true, according to Arendt, in spite of the fact that the modern tradition marks the rediscovery of the *vita activa* after centuries of subservience to the *vita contemplativa* of Plato and Christianity. For the modern tradition extols not action and politics, but the life of labour (satisfaction of needs and wants) and work (fabricating things and objects).

At the same time the ideals which characterized the birth of the modern age in the seventeenth century were, and continue to be, essentially economic and materialistic. Wedded to the ideals of progress and happiness, the modern spirit is fundamentally hostile to the life of true citizenship. To the extent that they were deeply commited to personal happiness, even the Romantics shared this spirit despite their hostility to progress. Liberalism, its ancient constitutional roots notwithstanding, and Marxism with its evident hatred of material inequality, are at bottom theories of materialism, not ideals of political citizenship. The end of these theories is just distribution of material goods, either according to merit or need. Liberalism and Marxism constitute and create, in their different ways, the materialistic spirit of the modern age.

For Arendt, citizenship and the claims of politics do not figure at all in the *essential* calculations of classical and modern thought on politics. The claims of politics as she understands them come to life again in her hands;

indeed they form a kind of resilient and confident intellectual structure inspiring her thoughts. In her view, at the root of politics lies the notion of freedom as public action in speech and deed between citizens. The aim of politics is to provide a public space in which citizens can act excellently and reveal themselves as individuals in their action. In short, politics at its best is the arena of heroic action and as such it necessarily entails deliberate contempt for private household and social interests. These interests denature the public spirit and the public sensibility which demand courage and virility. The "private" and the "natural" encourage cowardice and fear of public action. In Arendt's view, they induce a false pride in mere survival in much the same way as canons of absolute morality serve to inculcate a reverence for meekness and politeness. Great works and deeds cannot issue from a spirit harnessed to bodily needs or the perpetual fear of Hell.

Arendt's ideal of true citizenship is austere and demanding; economic and moral concerns do not play a part in her politics, at least not directly. This is the case because she believes that these interests, if allowed to dominate politics, will pervert it. Men can live together as a *moral* and *human* community, as we shall see, only when absolute morality and material concerns are not allowed to shape the tenor and the temper of politics. Politics divested of the entreaties of the body and conscience will in the long run serve the true moral and material interests of men better. Though Arendt's ideal of politics is anti-utopian, in that it stresses the importance of limits in politics, the claims that she makes on its behalf are unusually comprehensive: properly understood and practised, politics offers a forum for individuality, articulates reality in human life, provides the foundation of community and facilitates the achievement of human excellence. In the special sense in which Arendt understands them, none of these tenets is an explicit part of the political philosophy of the leading thinkers in the tradition, not even Aristotle.

Arendt's thought does not fit into any of the existing traditions. This is not at all surprising when we consider the fact that her thought traces its roots to an historical period which all traditions commonly depict as deficient in crucial respects. She rightly sees that these traditions hinder a proper understanding of and a proper respect for Periclean Athens. Their philosophical, moral and epistemological points of departure do not allow us to see the true significance, human meaning and political genius of this past. This is especially true of the classical and modern traditions of political theory.

Arendt is thus an anti-traditional thinker who nevertheless avails herself of insights threading the tradition, which illuminate her ideal of politics. Strains of the spirit of a number of thinkers in the tradition inform her writings, notably Aristotle, Machiavelli and in a certain sense Burke. From Aristotle's *Politics*, she derives her notion of the citizen, though she rejects his idea that the citizen's vocation is an ethical one. To Machiavelli Arendt is indebted for her understanding of public action, but she has no use for his celebration of material power and success. For Burke's sense of community (organic), she has great sympathy but she did not share his hostility to revolutionary change in politics. To describe Arendt as Aristotelian, Machiavellian or Burkean without substantive and major qualifications is a serious mistake: Arendt is Arendtian. Her way of looking at the world, at politics, and at man is new. What she has to say about political matters is unique and important. She drives home the truth that politics is not to be treated lightly: it harbours within its realm the seeds of our sense of reality, of excellence, freedom and, in a severely limited sense, morality of the kind appropriate to citizens who live together.

The thesis of this study is that Arendt is a political theorist in the sense in which Plato, Aristotle and Marx are theorists. In their writings there is to be found a comprehensive, consistent and resilient view of man, nature, society and politics, in the context of the human condition. Arendt is both less and more of a political theorist in some respects: less because she propounds no doctrine of the good life and the ultimate moral good, more because she is preoccupied with the public realm and public things with a passion unequalled in the tradition. Her theory is radical, novel, unusual and shocking but I contend that it is still political theory.

That is my general thesis. The specific thesis I wish to argue is that in her notion of the public realm lies the key to her political theory. To Arendt the public realm is a nearly sacred thing, the source of all that is the best and the brightest in the lives of men. The public realm is primary, everything else is secondary; this is the beginning and the end of her political theory. The significance and the relevance of the range of non-political claims on the common life of men are adjudged by her strictly from the viewpoint of the public realm. Thus in her political theory the private, the natural, the moral and the transcendent, including the higher reaches of the realm of the mind, appear as peripheral phenomena unfit for public display or public concern.

This judgement makes sense only from the viewpoint of the public realm and its peculiar standards. The same is true of other controversial judgements which characterize her thought, from her critique of Marx to her novel thesis on Eichmann. On each and every fundamental political and moral question, Arendt deployed her critical intellect from the point of view of the public realm. Failure to understand the special terrain of her public realm, and the "public" sensibility informing it, more or less ensured the disastrous misreading and misunderstanding which shadowed her writings. The plain fact is that Arendt can neither be understood nor subjected to *intelligent* criticism unless one penetrates her political theory to its core: her singular notion of the public realm.

The one incontestable point about political theory is that it is an argument in favour of public life, varying in strength, naturally, from theory to theory. That is reason enough to take political theory seriously since civilized life presupposes some form of public life. But when there is a widespread feeling that contemporary public life is in disarray, without intelligible purpose and destitute in civility and humanity, that is all the more reason to heed political theory. Arendt's political theory deserves attention purely on intellectual grounds: it is a provocative and reflective discourse on politics and the human condition. In the present circumstances, however, her political theory is nearly indispensable. For she is preoccupied with these very issues: the nature of the public realm, the relationship between the private and the public realm, the place of morality in public life and so forth.

No theorist in recent times can rival the tenacity and the intelligence with which Arendt confronted and engaged the crisis of contemporary public life. Whether or not one agrees with her analysis, it can hardly be denied that her political theory deserves serious consideration. Arendt postulates a new understanding of politics and the public realm and of the crucial link between personal identity and the public realm. Her thoughts on these matters are immensely relevant to both the public and private lives of modern men. Therein lies her critical significance and importance as a political theorist.

The reading of Arendt which this study proposes seems to be best able to make sense of her political writings. This reading will also establish certain criteria for understanding as well as judging her political theory. In view of the unusual nature of her political theory, however, a fair bit of ground has to be cleared before one can launch into the theory itself. This study therefore begins with a chapter on the precise and legitimate sense in which Arendt is a political theorist, followed by a critical discussion of her unusual method of argument.

The second chapter situates her theory *vis-à-vis* the tradition of political theory and traces the origins of her political theory and its peculiar disposition. The third chapter unravels Arendt's view of the human condition and the place of man and the public realm in it. The fourth chapter critically penetrates her theory of the public realm and the impulses animating it. The final chapter considers the relationship between the public realm and the claims of morality in terms of three instances of rending conflict drawn from her writings: the case of Billy Budd, the French Revolution, and the conduct of Eichmann. In each case Arendt made her judgements on the basis of her notion of the public realm. This, at least, is the burden of my argument.

No piece of writing is ever a purely personal accomplishment. The writer is indebted, in subtle and explicit ways, to other writers, teachers and friends. This study has benefited from the knowledge and influence of several generous spirits. To Ali Mazrui (Michigan) I owe my introduction to political theory. From Alkis Kontos, Ed Andrew, C. B. Macpherson, Peter H. Russell and Christian Bay (all of the University of Toronto), I have learned much about political theory and theorizing. To Christian and Peter, I am especially indebted for their intellectual guidance and friendship. In a difficult phase in the course of writing this book, Gregory Baum (McGill) was very helpful with his advice. I should like to thank him for his interest and concern.

For many years I taught political theory at the University of Calgary. To my colleague Shadia Drury, I am particularly indebted for her intellectual and personal companionship, and for her support of my writings on Arendt and other controversial subjects.

This study was shaped into its present form during my tenure as a post-doctoral Fellow in the Calgary Institute for the Humanities. For his unfailing understanding and encouragement, the Institute's director, Harold Coward, deserves special thanks. The director of Wilfrid Laurier University Press, Sandra Woolfrey, was equally supportive and I want to thank her as well.

Typing or word-processing is a taxing business: I wish to thank Gerry Dyer, Judi Powell and especially Ella Wensel, for the countless hours they spent transforming my scribblings into an elegant typescript. I should also like to thank Alison Bowes for proof-reading, and my editor at W.L.U. Press, Olive Koyama, for intelligent editing, and for putting up with my displays (infrequent) of authorial vanity.

To my parents, who are like myself recent immigrants, and who came to Canada late in their lives, I owe a debt that can never be fully repaid: they have stood by me through very trying circumstances. To Peggy O'Neil, I am also indebted in a personal way: she shared in and encouraged my first tentative pages on Arendt.

Finally, I want to acknowledge that this book has been published with the help of a grant from the Social Science Federation of Canada, using funds provided by the Social Sciences and Humanities Research Council of Canada. I should also like to thank the SSHRCC reader, Ron Preece of Wilfrid Laurier University, for his critical commentary on my manuscript.

Parts of Chapters 2 and 5 were published, respectively, in the *Canadian Journal of Political Science* (June 1980), *Philosophy and Social Criticism* (Fall 1982) and *Review of Politics* (April 1984).

Abbreviations

IN THIS STUDY, the following abbreviations have been used for the major works of Hannah Arendt.

HC   *The Human Condition* (New York: Doubleday, 1959)

OR   *The Origins of Totalitarianism* (Cleveland: Meridian, 1958; revised edition)

BPF   *Between Past and Future* (New York: Viking, 1968; enlarged edition)

EIJ   *Eichmann in Jerusalem* (New York: Viking, 1965; revised edition)

MDT   *Men in Dark Times* (New York: Harvest, 1968)

REV   *On Revolution* (New York: Viking, 1965)

VLE   *On Violence* (New York: Harvest, 1969)

CR   *Crises of the Republic* (New York: Harvest, 1972)

RAHEL   *Rahel Varnhagen* (New York: Harvest, 1974; revised edition)

LIFE   *The Life of the Mind* (New York: Harcourt, Brace, Jovanovich, 1978; published posthumously and edited by Mary McCarthy)

I & II   (Volume I — *Thinking*)
(Volume II — *Willing*)

JEW   *The Jew as Pariah* (edited and with an introduction by Ron H. Feldman; New York: Grove Press, 1978)

CHAPTER ONE

Hannah Arendt
as a political theorist

LITERARY POLITICAL THEORY

The most striking thing about Arendt's writing is the literary temper and
the associated sinuousness of her approach to human phenomena. This is a
matter of style as well as content. In reading her it soon becomes apparent
that the literary temper of her writing is of a piece with her thought:
Arendt's thinking is deeply imbued with and nourished by a love for the
meanings, ideals, sentiments and possibilities embedded in language,
especially public language, and the shaping role language plays in the
human construction of our social and political worlds, in the very conduct of
human relationships.

To describe her writing as literary entails a number of judgements about
the nature and the direction of her thinking. The most fundamental one is
that she makes no distinction between the literary and the political, an
identity she derives from her intimate knowledge of the ancient Greeks,
their political assumptions, manners and morals. She is to be understood as
saying that the ancient Greeks, especially the pre-Socratics, were right to
insist on the substantive unity of the literary and the political because
political action quintessentially is about the public use and deployment of
speech and language. For the ancient Greeks as well as for Arendt, the
phenomena of political life constitute a reality which can be grasped only in
the language citizens use in the public realm. Pericles' funeral oration
provides a forceful illustration, on one level, of the literary style and
ambition informing ancient Greek politics.

The link between the literary and the political is precisely evident in the
similarity of the passions which moved the Greek citizens to words and
deeds, to action, and those which drove the poets and the playwrights to the
dramatic stage. As Sophocles described it, the common root of the debates
in the *polis* and the declamations on the Athenian stage was the impassioned

---

Notes to Chapter One appear on page 15.

concern for "the dispositions that make civic life possible."[1] The identity of
the literary and the political was not of course literal: it was on the level of
attitude, on the plane of disposition. This point is worth stressing because
Arendt writes as if this identity is a literal one and because her thinking is
best understood as an architecture of particular dispositions towards politics, not as a literal statement about politics and the human condition.

Arendt's interest in the literary carries with it an associated insistence
on the concreteness of reality and a corresponding horror of the abstract. She
sees public life as a reality rarely susceptible to apprehension in concepts and
sophisticated ideologies. Both distort reality and, more importantly, make
it inaccessible to human understanding. The literary sense with its peculiar
feel for the immediate and the concrete is much more likely to yield reality
and a "realistic" grasp of reality than elaborate concepts and theories (in
their strict philosophical sense). Arendt came to see the latter as willed
creations of the mind imposed on the recalcitrant and fluid phenomena of
human and political life. There is something futile in this perspective
because her own investigation of the human condition and her political
theory bear the marks, necessarily, of conceptual and theoretical articulation. Nevertheless she wrote consciously as if she was in direct communion
with reality, unimpaired by dominating concepts and theories. That she
largely succeeded in this enterprise is evidenced by the curiously anti-
conceptual and anti-theoretical character of her concepts and theory. This is
borne out as well in her inveterate disdain for method and methodical
argument in her writings. She was moved not so much by disrespect for
method as by her conviction, learned from the poets and dramatists of
ancient Greece, that method produced no significant understanding of
reality, only a vindication of logic and consistency.

To depict Arendt's political theorizing as an exercise in Aristotelian
practical reason, as opposed to theoretical reason, is not illegitimate. Her
reservations about absolute claims to truth, her affinity for the concrete, and
her focus on action suggest a clearly practical bent. But it is equally crucial
to understand that the purpose of Arendt's practical reasoning is strikingly
different from that of Aristotle. For the latter, practical reason guides action
towards the morally right end, towards its *telos*. For Arendt, on the
contrary, there is no *telos*, no virtuous end, that impels her political actor:
his end is excellence in word and deed, in the performance, that recognizes
no moral obligations.

Arendt's literary temper, then, is of a piece with her settled antipathy to
the abstract and the methodical in understanding political life. To be
sensitive to the literary in the sense stipulated is to understand public life in
a manner contrary to that enshrined in the Western tradition of political

theory. In the latter part of this study it will become apparent how strong and entrenched was Arendt's disagreement with the perspectives and attitudes to politics characteristic of the tradition.

The literary sensibility is critically political inasmuch as literature is about the variousness, the complexity, and the difficulty of human relationships in the world. It is vitally about the rival possibilities for greatness and mediocrity, meaning and meaninglessness, worthiness and the worthlessness, reality and illusion, in the most comprehensive of our shared worlds, the political world. Literature above all is the act of discovering this world and its meaning. In its larger human sense this is the master or the primary world, and this is what Arendt calls our shared "space of appearance." Her political world has little to do with the narrow politics of power, gain and advantage: it is a world which is literary in its passions and concerns. A reader not conversant with literature nor alive to the literary in life cannot begin to understand her thinking on politics and its relationship to the non-political world. Not to be equipped with this knowledge is to inevitably misread and misunderstand her. Her writing on even the most serious matters often reads like a sensitive literary tale, a story of how it all began, where it might end and what it may all mean.[2]

The nature of her political theory is unusual and problematic precisely because of its origin in the peculiar literary milieu which nourished ancient Greek thought and politics. Indeed many of the difficulties of substance, of definition, and of argument which characterize her writings derive in large measure from her literary approach to human phenomena. To understand these difficulties is also to begin to understand the unique character, direction, and importance of her political theory. First, though, it is essential to grasp that Arendt *is* a political theorist in the essential senses of this term, and she is one in the grand tradition of political theory from Plato to Marx.

To be clear about the general meaning of political theory is a necessary prerequisite. In my view,[3] a political theory is first of all an argument about the *public* life of men in this world. The nature of this public life is a different, though by no means an irrelevant, question. Still, the term public must be understood to cover the range of concerns citizens have in common, concerns which necessitate and merit joint decision and action. The crucial point is that a theory which does not take seriously the notion of the public or civic realm is not a political theory. Second, a political theory must presuppose that public life is essential to what is deemed to be quintessentially human, on any reasonable definition of what it means to be human. In this sense political theory must see shared, public life as worthy of rational beings, as fulfilling some essential needs of men. Political theory is an argument not merely about survival but about living in a worthy and meaningful manner. This is the reason why liberal political theory, at least in its Hobbesian version, is sometimes denied the status of *political* theory.[4]

Third, a political theory should be genuinely theoretical: it must articulate a particular view of the relationship between politics and the condition of man, the place of man in this equation, and the purpose or the end of political life. Political theory must be normative, it must be "moral,"[5] and it must include a notion of human nature. Thus to count as political theory, an argument must be about the public relationships of men, must believe them to be essential to human life, and must concern itself, to some degree, with the larger questions of purpose and meaning that men invariably raise and seek to answer.

In my judgement, these three characteristics serve as adequate criteria for determining whether a particular work is or is not a piece of political theory in the general sense. Some theories may qualify more easily on one ground than on another. Others may qualify weakly on all three criteria. Be that as it may, a political theory must exhibit in a significant way these three elements. This of course still leaves open the question of definition of terms like "public," "normative," "human nature," and so on. What is to count as public, theoretical, or truly human is not and cannot be a settled issue.[6] Indeed the tradition of political theory is replete with keen competition between theorists to advance their particular definitions as the true and legitimate ones. In spite of the unsettled nature of argument about political phenomena, there has never been much doubt about two things central to political theory: its public character and its comprehensive intention. Both these elements are the specific legacy of Aristotle, although they were certainly present in Plato and Homer; Aristotle's famous descriptions of man as a political being and of politics as "the most comprehensive master science" underscore these elements in the nature of political theory.[7]

In these terms Arendt is and should be understood as a political theorist: this is one of the major contentions of this study. Her writings are first and most noticeably concerned, even obsessed, with public things, public phenomena, public men, public meaning, as the primary order of human business. Secondly, there is in what she says a keen literary appreciation of the sheer joy, happiness and feelings of self-worth which accrue to those who participate in the public business, to those who choose to become citizens. She makes it unequivocally clear that the public business is the true human business; those who abstain from it, for whatever reason, remain outside the pale of true humanity. In due course we shall see how this judgement is applied ruthlessly to some Africans and to some Jews.

And thirdly, Arendt is truly theoretical in her intention, in the manner of a Plato or a Marx. Her theory rests on a peculiar view of man, his place in the human condition and the significance of his political endeavours in the larger scheme of Nature. But there is an additional dimension to her thought which puts her squarely in the company of great political theorists. And this is the fact noticed by historians of political theory, that all great theories of the past arose during periods of general breakdown, political disarray and moral lostness: great political theory was born in a climate of uncertainty and widespread derangement in the world. The problem confronting the would-be theorist was not technical or partial, but total and "truly theoretical."[8] From Plato to Marx, all the great theorists in the tradition saw their arguments as ways of accounting for and transcending the attendant crises, in new orders based on different and better principles or, at least, principles which would more readily ensure order or justice or liberty. They put forward new theories to replace the old which they took to be mistaken or plainly wrong in light of the new circumstances.

Classical political theory is in this sense historical, in that it seeks to explain the causes of present disorder, and theoretical in that it offers a vision of the "good" life which is timeless and trans-historical. That is one part of the intention of the theorist. No less important is the theorist's parallel intention to correct or refute his predecessor(s) as Locke set out to improve upon the theory of Hobbes. More generally, most theorists in the tradition have intended their theories as legitimate contributions to the mode of discourse we call political theory.[9] This is the reason it is possible to speak of a tradition, because a tradition must necessarily share common intellectual concerns or it ceases to be a tradition.

A third element in the structure of the theorist's intentions has to do with the scope of his claim. Some theorists have asserted the utter novelty of their political arguments: Hobbes' insistence on this point is notorious. What is crucial to stress here is the decisive shift in Hobbes' concern away from the public to the private sphere of life. In this case the claim of utter novelty carried with it the demand to re-think and re-define the political in a startlingly new way. But Hobbes did not cut all the cords linking his theory to the traditional concerns of political theory. The public realm was still understood by Hobbes as central to politics even though it was deprived of many of the attributes it had enjoyed in earlier political theory. The radical character of Hobbes' theory had a severely practical and moral aim: to arrest the march of the state of nature, the spectre of civil war. Hobbes never ceased to fear the ever-present threat of the war of all against all. In his theory he sought to permanently eradicate the causes of turmoil and conflict.

In a similar manner, Arendt's political theory takes as its critical point of departure the advent of totalitarianism in Europe. Inevitably this fact had a personal bearing, in that the fate of the German Jews and of Jews generally was inseparably tied to that of Nazism. She responded to this event first as a Jew, as a member of a persecuted minority, not as a *human being*, at least not initially. To have claimed to be responding as a *human being* would have been both absurd and a lie, since the Jews were neither regarded nor treated as human beings.[10] Her earlier essays[11] and especially *The Origins of Totalitarianism*, are the impassioned products of the mind of a learned and sensitive Jew bravely grappling with the circumstances of her persecution and the origins of Nazi totalitarianism. In these works she writes self-consciously as a Jew, and it is perfectly legitimate to see her Jewish experience as shaping both the choice of issues and the tone of her work. During this period, 1933-1950, when her ideas on Jews and the Jewish catastrophe took root, she was and wished to be known as a Zionist, as an advocate and supporter of a Jewish homeland.[12] Though she eventually distanced herself from political Zionism, she still wanted and continued to fight instead for a Jewish homeland in a *secular* state in Palestine.[13]

There is no doubt then about the Jewish origin of some of her intellectual and political concerns. But she soon moved away from her exclusive concern with Jewish issues to writing as a human being whose concerns transcended the narrow interests of any group or community, including her own. She began to think and write as a theorist in the grand sense, and as such her interest in Jewish issues *as* Jewish issues declined. She now looked upon all issues, Jewish and non-Jewish, as human issues. From about 1952 onwards the Jews as Jews ceased to be central to her thought. She cultivated a degree of deliberate detachment with respect not only to Jewish issues but also to many of the characteristic ideas and motifs of the Western tradition of political theory, particularly its modern part. To Arendt it became clear that the degrading predicament in which the European Jews had found themselves posed a critical challenge to a tradition which had not anticipated nor could account for the shocking excesses of Nazi totalitarianism. A political theory, forthright and unsentimental, was called for in these new times: the "dark times." Hannah Arendt decided to answer that call.

Thus it is wrong to describe Arendt as a "uniquely *Jewish* thinker."[14] Her Jewishness cannot be said to be the *essence* of her thoughts, sentiments and ideals. Furthermore, her views on Jewish questions had little in common with those of establishment Jewry and its representatives.[15] To see her as a Jewish thinker, no more, no less, is to detract from her novelty and originality as a political theorist, and to minimize the scope and the strength of her disagreement with official Jewish organizations. On the other hand, Ron Feldman is right to insist that "Our understanding of her work . . . is diminished" if we remain ignorant of the "Jewish element" in her thought. But he as well is mistaken in believing that our grasp of her thought will be "seriously distorted if we overlook it."[16] One does not have to be a Jew or be aware of the fact that she was a Jew to understand, appreciate and evaluate her work in an intelligent manner. The sentiment of parochialism implied in this claim would have shocked and filled her with despair. This is not meant to suggest that Arendt remained totally "impartial" and "objective" about her own people. She was faithful in her personal way to her people. As we shall see, she was pained much more by the misfortunes of her own people than those befalling other minorities. In this respect, she proved ultimately to be "human, all too human." The attempt however to reclaim her not only as a "good" Jew but as a "uniquely Jewish thinker" would certainly have provoked her to object.

As a Jew, Arendt understood Nazi totalitarianism largely, though not exclusively, as a German-Jewish problem, even a European problem. But as a thinker she began to see the nature and the consequences of this event as more far-reaching and more challenging than anyone had imagined. To her, totalitarianism presented a truly human and a "truly theoretical" problem: this event signalled to her the reversal of all known values, the more or less complete moral and political collapse of the European world and society, derangement of the most thorough and cruel kind. This was indeed "murder most foul:" methodical mass murder committed in the line of normal civic duty. Why had it happened? How could it have been allowed to happen? What did it mean for man and his future? From her thoughtful and reflective answers emerged the outlines and eventually the elusive substance of what may properly be called her political theory. This theory is tentative and uncertain in some respects, and assertive and peremptory in others: it combines a high degree of immensely confident pronouncements with a considerable measure of substantive flexibility. In short, it is a political theory that is literary in the best sense: insightful, illuminating, occasionally mundane and all in all refreshing in its unconventionality and patrician boldness.

But that is not all. She claimed that the irruption of totalitarianism had put an end to Western theory and Western politics by the utter novelty of its thought and its practice: the Western kingdom had been torn asunder from within. She saw this event as presenting a uniquely theoretical and political problem. The main story of the West, which had begun with Plato and almost ended with Marx, had now finally come to a close. The tradition was broken, politics trampled, and freedom lost under the totalitarian assault of Hitler and Stalin. She would tell us what had happened and how it had happened. But it was a new story, a story without precedent because it was the story not only of the murder of many men but also the murder of all or most of our standards of judgement and understanding. She would also tell us or at least point to where some of the buried treasure could be found, and how this would help us to begin anew, to start our new politics. But to do that presupposes that we also know how things were and how they came to be in the political realm. To know the past is to understand the present and anticipate the future. Unlike Nietzsche she does not set herself against all traditions of political and moral thought. She does not believe, however, that these traditions have much to teach us about politics.

Arendt's intention as a political theorist is without parallel in the tradition. She does not mean only to correct and refute her predecessors, notably Marx among others: she claims that in one way or another, the entire tradition has been mistaken or wrong in its conception of politics. The thinking of the tradition on politics has been wrong in essential respects. This though does not stop her from appropriating elements of traditional thought which seem to her to be right or at least not wrong. Her intention then is theoretical and comprehensive in the most ambitious sense of these terms. Her writings taken together constitute a new view of politics. It is in this sense that she is not only a political theorist but a theorist of classical calibre. Sheldon Wolin[17] has convincingly argued that many of the theorists in our tradition should be understood, and are best understood, as creators of new paradigms of political theory. Marx, Hobbes and Plato were theorists of such stature: each one was confronted with wholesale derangement in his respective world; each one created a new theory to meet, understand and transcend the crisis, and in the process each one isolated a set of problems and puzzles which became uniquely associated with the names of these theorists. In sum, Marx, Plato and Hobbes created paradigms which put forward particular views of politics, of political theory and the kind of problems worth considering.

Taking Wolin's portrait of the tradition as my starting point, I want to suggest that Arendt is the creator of a paradigm which is certainly new, but also radically different. The paradigm creators in the tradition had one fundamental characteristic in common: they were all talking about essentially the same things: the institutional arrangement of power, law and order, security of life and property, all this incorporated in some particular conception of justice and the good life as the essence of politics. The task of political theory was to elaborate and defend the ultimate ground of the relationship between man and the State in political society. Arendt is barely interested in these basic phenomena of politics. For that matter her interest in the structures and institutions of society like the State, government, family, law, parties, and party-systems, is almost non-existent. When she does address these elements she restricts herself to making insubstantial assertions which are not open to theoretical or historical scrutiny. She is evidently not interested in the conditions of political order or the concrete dimensions of political offices. In spite of her repeated insistence on the concrete in political life, the actual institutions and practices of everyday politics do not engage her attention. She takes these things for granted: no politics can exist without these regularized institutions and practices. For Arendt however this is politics at its most mundane. There is nothing here which is really unique, worthwhile or surpassing as a statement of true *humanitas*.

In contrast to the theorists in the tradition, Arendt's attention is fixed elsewhere. Her politics are the politics of drama and proud ambition. She is moved to extravagant eloquence by public words and deeds between citizens. She is capable of austere praise and nobility of sentiment only when she is speaking of Achilles in battle, of citizens in Homeric contest in the public arena. Arendt is not merely at odds with the extant traditions of politics and political thought, she is opposed to the very ideals of politics which underscore the main traditions: classical, modern, Christian, liberal and Marxian. This does not make her thought hopelessly "idiosyncratic,"[18] but it certainly makes it extremely difficult and helps explain her marginality in the recent history of political theory. Her marginality became canonical inasmuch as it became evident that her original political theory, understood as a discourse on the human condition, also entailed an implicit but scathing attack on the modern mind and the modern sensibility: on its methods, its scholarship, its ideals, and its pride in its grasp of reality.

Like all paradigm-creators, Arendt proposes a new reading of politics, the nature of the political, and the task of political theory. Her reading is remarkable for not only what it excludes but also for what it includes as essential to politics, properly understood. To explicate this reading, carefully and critically, is the purpose of this study. From the outset, it is necessary to understand two crucial points about her thinking. First, Arendt wrote not only as a political theorist but also as a sensitive and learned woman trying to comprehend the manners, the morals, the interests, and the ideals of classical and modern men. Her political theory is not simply there to be picked, nor is it set out in her *Republic* or her *Leviathan*: it has to be literally unearthed and sifted from her wide-ranging writings, and then cast into an argument about politics.

Second, because her political theory is to an unusual degree literary in many of its substantive concerns, it has to be approached with considerable care and intelligence, in the serious manner of the literary figures who have addressed her thought: W. H. Auden, Mary McCarthy, Robert Lowell, Randall Jarrell, Alfred Kazin and Stephen Spender, among others. This of course is not to say that she is therefore to be deemed immune to criticism of the usual sort, but it is to insist that she makes stringent demands on her readers and on those who would write on her.

For what Arendt has done is to invent a new genre of writing and reflection which lies somewhere between political theory in its usual sense and literary criticism. Perhaps "invent" suggests too much originality. There is, however, a striking originality in an approach which persuades and enables one to see meanings, ideas and realities in politics not ordinarily thought to be part of the political realm. She casts politics and the public realm in a new light, as newly significant for the common affairs of men. In view of the peculiar literary nature of her political theory it would be unwise to see it as a substitute for traditional normative theory or modern empirical research. Her achievement was of a different order, which she unarguably intended as a massive corrective to what she saw as serious lacunae in the traditional conception of politics. But the nature of her theoretical accomplishment is such that it does not enable us to dismiss the classical tradition. Indeed it cannot, because Arendt put forth no doctrine of the good life, no injunctions against wrongdoing and no principles of justice and moral right. Her ideal vision of politics is devoid of interdictory restraints, disallowing certain kinds of actions as harmful and dangerous *a priori*. Her political theory is critically wanting in this respect. This study will address her originality as well as the morally troubling thrust of her political theory.

METHOD AND IMAGINATION

Though immensely learned and a scholar, Arendt is much more than that. She is a thinker, an intellectual in the non-academic sense, a woman with new and important ideas. She did not set out to be a scholar in the narrow sense of correctly interpreting Marx, Plato or Rousseau. She did not intend to become a professional scholar, one equipped with the proper scientific method, who had her "three-by-fives in order," and who knew how to do "research."[19]

Her criticism, interpretation and reflection upon events, ideas and thinkers past and present are only secondarily instances of scholarship and erudition. They are primarily the materials of *her* text and *her* theory of man and politics. This text, this theory and its meaning have largely been ignored because of the impoverished attitude towards her work. The crucial first step in understanding Arendt is to engage her in the spirit of those who wish to learn. Scholarly criticism and judgement must come later. To say this is perhaps to make too neat and rigid a distinction between understanding and scholarly criticism. Rather what is required is an intelligent and sensitive form of scholarship which combines understanding and criticism. The critical scholarly impulse in short must respect the equally pressing scholarly obligation to understand the writer on her own ground, on the special terrain she has carved out for her inquiry. The writer's text has to be seen and understood in her peculiar context.

Two critics in particular have addressed the context of Arendt's writing with intelligence and sensitivity. Sheldon Wolin has remarked the poor state of political debate and political theory in the United States prior to the publication of Arendt's *The Origins of Totalitarianism* and *The Human Condition*. Until then much of political theory or what passed for political theory was "neither political nor theoretical." Her work contributed significantly to setting the terms of the ensuing theoretical debate about the meaning and the ends of political life in a new and an unstable era.[20] In his fascinating memoir *New York Jew*,[21] Alfred Kazin recounts the paucity of serious debate, in the post-war period, about the tragic political events the world had just witnessed. The academics of various ideological persuasions did not have much to say about the Holocaust, "about the gas." The learned were silent on these serious matters. In this climate of diffidence and indifference, writes Kazin, emerged Arendt with her arresting book on totalitarianism: here was a writer neither of the left nor of the right, well versed in literature, philosophy and the nuances of politics, iconoclastic and unclassifiable, who addressed herself seriously, thoughtfully, independently and indeed passionately to the central events of this century.[22]

It is difficult to overestimate the importance of a thinker actually attending to the critical moral and political problems of this age; of a writer actually *doing* political theory, instead of paying academic homage once again to a Plato or a Rousseau, to the great tradition. Her work went beyond it to open a new window or two. She deliberately refused to become another student of the great tradition and stop there. Instead, she learnt it, appropriated it and creatively applied it to new problems and new dilemmas. She reworked elements of the tradition to illuminate the past and the present. In the words of *The New Yorker*, she was "one of those thinkers, rare in all history, who are empowered to inch human thought forward."[23]

"To be with Hannah Arendt," Kazin tells us, "was to learn and learn." Those eager to learn included poets Randall Jarrell, Robert Lowell, W. H. Auden, Stephen Spender, philosopher Hans Jonas, novelist Mary McCarthy, publisher William Jovanovich, psychologist Bruno Bettelheim, historian Salo Baron, and Kazin himself.[24] All of them even in disagreement respected the calibre of mind and the striking intelligence she brought to bear on problems of immediate and public concern. This is the attitude most appropriate in reading Arendt.

Still, one can sympathize with busy scholars confronted with an original writer who is also exasperating in her method of argument. In fact, the terms "method," "argument," and "analysis" are not readily applicable to Arendt's work, lacking as it is in a methodical approach, proper analysis and, in particular, lacking in arguments of the sort we have come to expect from political theorists and students of political theory. This is essentially true of almost all of her writings and especially true of her last work, *The Life of the Mind*. She is a difficult thinker *and* difficult to understand because she offers no arguments as such, only intimations and reflections, often just assertions, which point in a certain direction. Bernard Elevitch has rightly identified the striking characteristic of her thinking: Arendt's points are "*extended but not developed.*"[25] The result of this approach is that her thinking comes across as substantively slippery. Hence it has been easy for some to see in this approach an absence of true substance. This fundamental weakness has tended to encourage facile comprehension and also to obscure her essential theory and its larger significance as a political and moral argument.

Philosopher Brand Blanshard had this to say about *The Human Condition*:

The meat of this thoughtful book is as hard to extract as the meat of a hickory nut. It is encased in complicated sentences, whose many clauses and qualifications seem meant to guard their secret against any but the most determined attack.[26]

Such judgements about the nature of her thought are shared by many philosophers, including J. M. Cameron, Charles Frankel, Eric Voegelin and Ernst Vollrath. Frankel notes that her political and philosophical positions were neither defined nor defended; that they were based on a "metaphysics" which she had not bothered to spell out, then or later.[27] Cameron complains about her "opacity of style" and "darkness of thought." Eric Voegelin, not renowned for the clarity of his prose, remarks on her unclear and unspecified method of political and historical analysis.[28] In his thoughtful essay on her, Vollrath rightly argues that it may be "a misguided premise to speak of method"[29] in discussing her work.

To serious critics, this lack of structure and clarity can hardly come as a surprise, given Arendt's new and strange manner of understanding political phenomena and her settled disregard for proper argument in support of her claims. To make matters worse, she disdained disciplinary boundaries in her writings: she drew without inhibition from the wells of philosophy, etymology, ethics, history, theology, economics, philosophy of science, cultural studies, biology, literature and her own personal experience as if these fields were of a piece, and she moved with enviable facility from one to the other, often in the space of a single essay, sometimes in the same paragraph in her writing. She was also disinclined to observe intellectual and social chronology in her writing.

In stressing all this, my point is that Arendt fashioned her own relevant past out of the Western past and shaped it into the pertinent context of her thoughts and her ideas. The figures in the tradition whom she praises or dismisses are summoned before us not to do them "scholarly" justice but to play a part in *her* story and *her* theory. This should not be understood to mean that she wilfully misrepresented or even misunderstood a Plato or a Marx. She looked at these figures, instead, in a new and not always clear light, as thinkers who had something important to say about *her* central concerns and *her* standpoint on man and politics. *Her writings make sense on the basis of her unique perspective which cannot be assimilated to extant traditions, even with those upon which she leans quite heavily.*

Since she used no particular method and since she did not espouse a particular tradition *in toto*, how did she come to write on the issues she did, and how did she come to write in the manner she did? The first thing to be said is that Arendt wrote and theorized a great deal from personal experience which, in her case, was also political experience. She did not of course present her raw experience as serious political theory, but it is quite true to say that her political theory is inconceivable without her personal experience. This experience provided the impulse and the substantive thrust of her thinking about political matters. And because her experience was born of political turmoil and because it brought her face to face with human unfreedom and mass murder, she tended to think and write as if politics, human affairs, and freedom were identical phenomena. Thus her inability and unwillingness to separate the one from the other. This is but the beginning of her stridently non-academic approach to politics and human affairs.

Secondly, she relied in large measure on the faculty of imagination, distinguishing it from fancy, fantasy and ordinary irrationality. In one of her early essays, "Understanding and Politics," Arendt defended imagination in the language of Wordsworth as "Reason in her most exalted mood."[30] She saw imagination as the mental ability peculiarly suited to the study of politics and history because these subjects, as she understood them, depended for their substance and meaning on the human mind's capacity to reason beyond reason. Without saying so explicitly, she was invoking a pre-modern understanding of reason as entailing an interpretive ability which transcended the modern view of reason as the domain of logic and utilitarian calculation. Arendt did not merely mean that the faculty of imagination was a necessary adjunct to social science methods of analysis and argument; she defended imagination as better and more appropriate than scientific method and empirical research, in the study of human and political phenomena.[31] It is not an exaggeration to say that her thought is directly and indirectly a conscious attack on the battery of modern social science methods as poor and weak instruments of analysis and understanding. She came to believe that contemporary social and political theories based on these methods misrepresented politics, and failed to distinguish between the significant and the insignificant in the realm of political and moral issues.[32] Indeed it is a contention of this study that Arendt's thinking, in spite of its studied disregard of modern method and argument, sheds far more light on the nature and the meaning of political life and its importance for human life than many social science texts learned in the latest methods of research and scientific analysis.[33]

Arendt's antipathy to modern and contemporary methods of political science is by no means arbitrary, although she did not argue her point of view with care. Her few remarks on this topic in her writings, together with her literary disposition towards human affairs, make the claim that the kind of attitude and intellectual interest presupposed in these methods is incapable of yielding a true grasp of politics and political life.[34] Vollrath's perceptive essay is worth recalling here. He argues that Arendt's "political thinking does not posit itself *a priori* outside the political field; rather it grows from within the field."[35]

Vollrath is right, but it needs to be emphasized that, despite her fidelity to the phenomena of politics, she did not allow herself to be carried along indiscriminately by the flow of political life. She certainly maintained her distance from and assumed a position towards politics; her theory reveals a sharply normative point of view, critical yet faithful to politics.

The kind of political thinking she practised implicitly postulated the unargued argument, that political theory must not and ought not seek to rise too far above the phenomena it encounters or to subdue the phenomena it studies. Arendt's highly critical stance towards methods and theories is based on her conviction that they interfere with the realities and the truths of political life if they are used, as they invariably are, as devices for stringently ordering, managing, and ultimately controlling political life.

For the interpreter or critic of her political theory, Arendt's settled lack of interest in method and methodical argument poses a serious scholarly problem. Her thinking does not lend itself to the kind of exegesis that scholars practise on the political thought of, say, Aristotle or Hobbes or even Marx. The nature of her concepts is such that it does not allow *a traditional scholarly performance* on the part of the interpreter. Her concepts are as a rule fluid and unstable, so that even the "most determined attack" (Blanshard's phrase) will encounter its share of difficulties, in much the same way in which such difficulties beset an interpreter of Nietzsche or Heidegger. In a sense the problem is worse with Arendt because she is, as I have argued, a political theorist who understood herself as writing within the tradition of discourse described as political theory. Neither Nietzsche nor Heidegger did or could make such a claim.

To recognize the novelty of her approach is also to notice the perhaps most crucial thing about Arendt's thinking: that finally the moral sensibility and the intellectual thrust of her political theory are much more important than the individual ideas. Stated differently, it is the forest rather than the trees that embodies her singular vision, even though many a tree sparkles with extraordinary energy. To forestall misunderstanding: the parts obviously deserve attention, but in the context of her political theory and its larger purpose.

Arendt's "method" is thus much less a method and much more an attitude, a singular disposition to politics and human life. That this disposition has particular sources and a particular direction does not render her political theory any less difficult as an argument. Her refusal to heed any method and her insistence that political theory had to rediscover its original impulse, long buried in the tradition and traditional thinking, made it possible for her to encounter and confront the really important issues of this age with intelligence and with courage that no other contemporary political theorist of her calibre has been able to match. Both Leo Strauss and Eric Voegelin were deeply concerned with the challenge posed by modernity to the wisdom of the classical tradition. Yet in this particular sense, their great achievements seem politically marginal and morally trivial inasmuch as neither forthrightly tackled the concrete challenge of contemporary modernity: the challenge of totalitarianism to the nature and the meaning of politics.

NOTES

1 Quoted by D. S. Carne-Ross in his excellent essay, "Classics and the Intellectual Community," *ARION* 1, 1 (1973) (7-66): 41.

2 For a similar view, see Stan Draenos, "Thinking Without Ground: Hannah Arendt and the Contemporary Situation of Understanding" in *Hannah Arendt: The Recovery of the Public World*, ed. M. A. Hill (New York: 1979): 220.

3 This view owes much to the sensitive and learned writings of Sheldon Wolin: *Politics and Vision* (Boston, 1960); "Political Theory as a Vocation" in the *American Political Science Review* (Dec. 1969), pp. 1062-1082, and "Paradigms and Political Theories" in *Politics and Experience: Essays Presented to Michael Oakshott*, ed. P. King and B. C. Parekh (Cambridge, 1968): 125-152.

4 See for example Sheldon Wolin, *Politics and Vision*, Ch. 9. Wolin also includes Locke in this category. Leo Strauss in his *Natural Right and History* (Chicago, 1953) makes a similar argument but on the basis of different premises: Ch. 5.

5 In this context the term moral here means that a political theory recommends and justifies certain values as primary: See George Kateb, *Political Theory* (New York, 1968), pp. 2-3.

6 See Wolin, *Politics and Vision*: 1 and 5.

7 *Nichomachean Ethics* (Indianapolis, 1962): 4.

8 Wolin, "Political Theory as a Vocation:" 1980.

9 For a critical discussion of this point see John G. Gunnell, *Political Theory: Tradition and Interpretation* (Cambridge, 1979), Ch. II, esp. 52-53.

10 See *MDT*: 17-18.

11 The most important ones have been collected in *JEW*.

12 On this point see Ron Feldman in *JEW*: 16.

13 *JEW*: 191, 192 and 247. Though she had severe differences with the Zionists as early as 1944, she did not break with them until after the creation of Israel. Then there was no longer any doubt that Israel would be an *exclusivist Jewish state*. For a critical discussion of this issue, see my essay "Hannah Arendt on Political Zionism" in *Arab Studies Quarterly* (Summer 1986).

14 Leon Botstein, "Hannah Arendt: The Jewish Question" in *The New Republic* (Oct. 21, 1978): 34 (emphasis added). In this essay Botstein attempts, unsuccessfully I think, to discover a Jewish basis to almost all her ideas: 32-37.

15 Her exchange with Scholem brings this out with utmost clarity; cf. *JEW*: 240-251.

16 See *JEW*, Introduction: 20, and footnote 3: 48.

17 "Paradigms and Political Theories," in *Politics and Experience*: 125-152.

18 Margaret Canovan, *The Political Thought of Hannah Arendt* (London: 1974): 121.

19 D. S. Carne-Ross' "Classics and the Intellectual Community," *ARION*, 1973: 30-33, *passim*, is a learned and impassioned indictment of the professional and technical "research" that passes for scholarship these days.

20 "Hannah Arendt and the Ordinance of Time," *Social Research* (Spring 1977): 91-93.

21 (New York: 1978).

22 *New York Jew*: 298-300.

23 Dec. 22, 1975: 27.

24 *New York Jew*, 1978: 299.

25 "Hannah Arendt's Testimony," *Massachusetts Review*, Vol. XX, No. 2, Summer 1979: 373 (emphasis added).

26 *New York Times Books Review* (Feb. 15, 1959): 26.

27 *Political Science Quarterly* 74 (1959): 422.

28 *New York Review of Books* (Nov. 6, 1969): 68 and *Review of Politics* 15 (1953): 76.

29 "Hannah Arendt and the Method of Political Thinking," *Social Research* 44 (Spring 1977): 162.

30 *Partisan Review* 20 (Summer 1953): 392.

31 Arendt, "A Reply" (to Eric Voegelin), *Review of Politics* (Jan. 1953): 79-80; see also *OR*: 482 and *HC*: 40-42.

32 *HC*: 81; *BPF*: 49, 101-103; see also *VLE* which relentlessly criticizes modern methods and modern theories.

33 For a discussion of the poverty of contemporary social science, see Wolin, "Political Theory as a Vocation:" 1062-1078.

34 *MDT*: ix; *REV*: 9, 91.

35 "Hannah Arendt and the Method of Political Thinking," *Social Research*: 163.

CHAPTER TWO

Tradition and the past

TRADITION DOES NOT contain the "essence" of the past: it includes some but not all of the past.[1] By nature traditions necessarily exclude what is deemed irrelevant, insignificant or mistaken. Falling into this pattern, the Western tradition of political philosophy has excluded a salient chunk of its past and this excluded past is the truly *political* past. This is the remarkable and novel starting point of Hannah Arendt's political theory.

To be more exact, this is one strand in the complex origins of her political theory. The other two are her intellectual and personal encounter with Nazi totalitarianism and her discovery of the political genius of the pre-Socratic past. Her political theory originates in her attempt to make sense of totalitarianism and its consequences, in terms of knowledge about politics supplied by the tradition of political philosophy. But this tradition was unable to account for the totalitarian assault on politics: by its very practice the latter had transcended the traditional categories of good and bad regimes. This hard fact was the reason she thought it necessary to go "beyond" the tradition to Homer and Pericles, in search of answers to the oldest questions of political theory. Therein lie the seeds of Arendt's unique theory of politics and the public realm.

POLITICS AND POLITICAL THEORY

For Arendt the primary warrant for politics is human freedom, which is "ontologically rooted" in the fact of natality.[2] Politics is the practice of civic life tempered by an elegant sensibility to the claims of imagination and meaning. Without the fact of freedom neither politics nor human meaning is conceivable. In its factual and imaginative dimensions politics thrives on

---

Notes to Chapter Two appear on page 41.

the ground of freedom. Tirelessly Arendt repeats this theme in all her works.

If politics presupposes freedom, then political theory similarly depends on it. To be free is to be able to choose in both intellectual and factual terms. Hence political theory is a form of choice, an assertion of the freedom to choose. Arendt's political theory differs in style and substance from traditional political theory in its overriding emphasis on the public realm and public freedom. In her view the task of political theory is essentially to articulate, defend and celebrate the reality of human freedom. This freedom is political in the special sense that it is always public. Freedom is expressed and experienced only in the public realm, in the presence of fellow men, nowhere else. For Arendt freedom cannot exist in private. In her own words "the *raison d'être* of politics is freedom."[3]

In her writings the terms politics, public realm, and freedom often appear as synonymous. "Freedom" is the link between politics as normative practice and political theory as normative vision. In addition, within the bounds of the human condition, which is a shared condition, freedom and its exercise is the *human* good available to men. Viewed in this light the entire tradition of political theory fails to measure up to its appointed task: the articulation and the defence of public freedom. This "failure" lends to the tradition an air of political unreality. Indeed Arendt writes that this tradition "could easily be interpreted as various attempts to find theoretical foundations and practical ways for an escape from politics altogether."[4] Arendt succumbs in large measure to this temptation. From Plato to Marx, she contends, the denial of freedom and therefore of politics and the public realm has been the presiding impulse in the tradition.

Arendt's analysis of the tradition is unsystematic, sparse and often cryptic. In spite of the fact that she is also wont to pursue contradictory strands, her reading of this tradition is tolerably clear. What she has to say is both new and important, and relevant to understanding politics. For her, although she does not say it, this tradition is clearly divisible into the classical and the modern tradition. Machiavelli is a special case whose position and contribution will be discussed later in this study.

For Arendt the classical tradition begins with Plato's "turning away from politics and then returning in order to impose his standards on human affairs."[5] The immediate cause is the fate of Socrates. Understandably, a society which could condemn a man like Socrates to death had little to recommend it. The standards with which Plato returns to politics are standards antithetical to politics. They seek to arrest free action and impose a strict order inhospitable to freedom. In Plato, writes Arendt, originates a view of politics as irresponsible and immoral action. Furthermore, it is a view arrived at, not from experience in politics, but from the perspective of truth and right as ascertained by the philosopher. Thus the classical tradition is a *philosophic* tradition founded "explicitly in opposition to (the) *polis*."[6] Plato assumed that he had found not another principle to order human actions but "a higher principle" to rule the *polis*.[7] This higher principle was none other than moral virtue attained in contemplation of the Absolute Good. In this view politics becomes subordinated to the higher claims of the perfect moral life: it has no other aim than to make the philosophic-moral life possible.

In the Platonic conception, human action is associated with turbulence and uncertainty in society. Action itself is seen as the source of disturbance and discontent because action lacks the imprint of moral form. Men pursue interests and aims in society unhampered by any interdictory restraint. To arrest this state of affairs Plato demands "surcease . . . from activity" in the world.[8] Life in the *polis* is no longer to be one of worldly pursuits but one organized for the attainment of moral virtue. For Arendt the upshot of this argument is that political activity is now to be counted, together with labour and work, among the necessities of life. Here politics has been deprived of its claim to constitute an authentic way of life—a claim central to the Athenian *polis*.

This is one side of the new picture. The other is that politics is conceived in the image of fabrication so that all "action" affirms the guiding model at every stage. This model is that of the contemplative-moral life as the highest life human beings can attain. For Plato politics becomes a creative art in the service of the higher end. In Plato the fundamental ends are rule and order, both of which preclude free action. Ironically, at its very start, the tradition of political theory attempted to rid the community of politics and to entirely eliminate action.

Even Aristotle, who was "much closer to current Greek opinion than Plato,"[9] and despite his sensitive appreciation of the ancient practice of politics, subordinated politics to the pursuit of moral virtue. According to Arendt, Aristotle's discovery of a hierarchy of goods in the human world did not prevent him from finally subsuming political life to moral life. While Aristotle maintains against Plato that politics is the best way of life in the world, he nevertheless conceives it as a means to the higher life of contemplation. Aristotle, no less than Plato, looks upon politics as ultimately epiphenomenal.

For Arendt the point is not that Plato and Aristotle doubted that "freedom is exclusively located in the political realm" or that they misunderstood the nature of politics.[10] Quite the contrary. Plato and Aristotle (more so) understood the intimate connection between politics and freedom only too well. They knew that it was to be found in the realm of human affairs but they despaired of the turbulence, the uncertainty, and the "moral irresponsibility" of politics and of its consequences. They were bothered by political action: "the unpredictability of its outcome, the irreversibility of the process and the anonymity of its authors."[11] These features of politics based on freedom and action served, in their view, to impede the attainment of a properly human life.

From Arendt's viewpoint the classical attempt to rid politics of freedom and action entails a revaluation of man *qua* political man (citizen). In her view "action alone is the exclusive prerogative of man."[12] And it is precisely this capacity for action which makes politics possible: "neither a beast nor a god," she writes, following Aristotle, "is capable of it."[13] In seeking to eliminate action from politics, Plato and Aristotle explicitly claim that the human capacity distinctive to men is not action but self-rule and its corollary rulership. For them man is not truly human because he can act and actualize his freedom, but because of his ability to ruthlessly rule himself and others—an ability that harbours the seeds of moral virtue and humanity. Freedom and therefore politics have no place in this equation. For Arendt it is this dual philosophic revaluation—of man and the purpose of politics—which accounts for the "apolitia" of the classical tradition.

From the start the classical tradition is anti-political in ethos. In it politics, no less than labour and work, is absorbed into and confined to the "cave:" politics is no more worthy than other activities and certainly not worthwhile in itself. To the extent that these activities have meaning, it is in relation to their contribution to the superior moral life.

For the modern tradition, on the other hand, Arendt has little use. In the main this tradition, which begins with Hobbes, celebrates neither freedom nor moral virtue but necessity: it is characterized—in Hobbes, Locke and Smith—by the pursuit of *natural* good. Politics here is subordinated to economics.[14] Hobbes, Arendt tells us, was the first in the tradition who oriented himself "according to the requirements of the political realm"[15] of his time. He was concerned not with politics but with "the needs of the new social body of rising bourgeoisie."[16] For Hobbes the requirements of the political realm were the requirements of a stable order, such as to allow the new "social body" to amass wealth and power. For Hobbes there is no such thing as a public interest separate from private interests. His commonwealth has one purpose and only one purpose: to allow men to pursue their private economic interests, the natural good. The power that Hobbesian man seeks is economic power, his "value or worth . . . his price"[17] in the marketplace.

For Hobbes politics is an idle luxury to be assiduously avoided: it interferes with the urgent business of living and competing for scarce natural goods. Consequently, in Hobbes there are no citizens, no men devoted to the "publique." Hobbes assumes that public good is the sum of private interests. The freedom that Hobbesian man wants is freedom from politics and freedom to gratify his needs and desires.

With Hobbes the life-process of biological necessity assumes unparalleled significance. The aim of this process is the relentless pursuit of material power. For Arendt it is this obsession with the process of life which defines the modern tradition. Stated differently, it is the sway of necessity in its most elementary manifestation—life itself—which rules this tradition. Even John Locke and Adam Smith, who were far more interested in politics than Hobbes, succumb to the image of man and society as a life-process ruled by necessity. For them as well politics is a function of society: it has the purpose of ensuring economic well-being.

Between the passion for life and its cares and the degradation of politics, Arendt thus sees an intimate connection. Where the concern for life is preeminent, necessity is triumphant. Even Hegel does not escape this verdict. Necessity reigns unchecked in his thought, but this time in the guise of historical necessity. For Arendt it is significant that in the unfolding of the historical process, as Hegel conceives it, it is the idea and ideal of necessity which lends meaning to human existence.[18] In this image of society, politics as freedom and action cannot but appear as epiphenomenal, unreal and accidental. For Hegel what is real is the process of history and historical development.

If for Hegel it is still spirit which is revealed and embodied in history, for Marx it is unequivocally crude economic necessity which characterizes human history. In Marx, writes Arendt, "the life-process is the very centre of human endeavour."[19] Biological need—the blunt necessity for bread— is at the core of Marx's interest. In Arendt's view, to put it in terms she does not use, Marx's critique of bourgeois economics is an argument against the capitalist monopoly of labour's fruits: it is *not* an attack on materialism or wealth nor an attack on labour *per se*. Marx's ideal, on the contrary, is an "abundance" of material wealth justly distributed. To Arendt, the primacy of material abundance in Marx is actually the reason why Marx sought to make the labouring activity philosophically respectable. In Marxian thought there occurs a dramatic revaluation of labour. Marx severs the age-old identification of labour and necessity. Far from expressing "subjection to necessity," labour in Marx, according to Arendt, "became the very expression of the humanity of man."[20]

In this context, it is important to note that Arendt recognizes that for Marx—at least in his younger days—man was a being "endowed with the faculty of action,"[21] a view derived from his perceptive understanding of Greek politics. Indeed, Arendt writes, Marx's "general and often inexplicit outlook was still firmly rooted in the institutions and the theories of the ancients."[22] But Marx's debt to Greek politics was effectively tempered by his need to explain and interpret the new industrial age. Thus Marx rediscovered the faculty of action but reduced it to necessity: Marx saw action as the metabolic interchange between men and nature. To Marx, it is not politics and freedom but labour and necessity which are fundamental. Here action is no more than an ancillary moment in the life-process.

In Arendt's interpretation Marx, no less than Hobbes, Locke and Smith, is ruled by the modern passion for natural good. Where nature and necessity rule, politics is not possible. For Arendt this is crucial, for no matter how one slices it, freedom and politics are possibilities against and beyond the claims of necessity and labour. Making labour the focus of freedom and humanity, as Marx did, simply confuses freedom with necessity, with the result that man no longer knows the distinction between being free and being under the whip of necessity. The modern venture radically reverses the traditional relationship between the *vita contemplativa* (life of the mind) and the *vita activa* (life of action) and correspondingly it revalues the *differentia specifica* of man. But for this reversal, according to Arendt, the domain of need and necessity would have remained a subsidiary concern.

In Plato and Aristotle *vita contemplativa* is unmistakably the superior way of life. *Vita activa* receives its meaning and "restricted dignity" from the *vita contemplativa* and only "because it serves the needs and wants of contemplation."[23] From the perspective of the *vita contemplativa* distinctions among activities are of no consequence. *Vita activa* thus appears to be of a piece. For Arendt, the primary claims of reason and moral virtue in the classical view ensure that the domain of needs and wants is circumscribed. Necessity remains bound to the moral standard of judgement inherent in the *vita contemplativa*. This standard in the classical view is not man but the transcendental Absolute Good.

In contrast, in the modern tradition the *vita contemplativa* did not just become subordinated to the *vita activa*, it was consigned to the unscientific dustbin of the past. For Arendt this was first evident in the thought of Hobbes where reason lost its roots in contemplation and became "a mere faculty of reckoning with consequences" of private aims.[24] In Hobbes what men desire is good and what they are averse to is bad: moral questions are useless vanities. These conclusions are not accidental in the thought of a man who "denounced all past philosophy as nonsense."[25]

Later, Hegel, according to Arendt, continued this trend by transforming "metaphysics into a philosophy of history."[26] Truth for Hegel, as for his student Marx, was found not in any suprasensual realm but in the midst of human affairs. The link between the real and the actual, rational and practical, between idea and fact became firmly established in the modern tradition. This innovation in thought, wrought by the modern thinkers, signals the demise of *vita contemplativa*. Once truth is located in the fluctuating realm of human affairs, contemplation as the pursuit of truth, and the associated capacities of reason and thought, can no longer function as in the past.

For Arendt the result of this revolution was that the *vita activa* liberated itself from restrictions binding upon the classical tradition: "contemplation . . . lost its position in the *vita activa* itself."[27] There were no standards of judgement, no restraining motifs to which men could appeal. Without a belief in at least the existence of unchanging truth there can be no sense of limits in human activity: only then could the domain of need violently assert itself, only then could it demand to rule human existence. For Arendt this is necessarily the case since *natural* man becomes the standard of his own activity, of what is good for him. From Hobbes to Marx, notwithstanding many differences, the ruling passion was "the force of the life process itself, to which all men and all human activities were equally submitted and whose only aim, if it had an aim at all, was the survival of the animal species man."[28] This is a strong claim and one meant to be taken in all seriousness.

In the modern tradition, the dominant image of man is that of natural man unrestrained by any transcendental barrier. Man seems to be no more than the best among beasts, distinguished neither by reason, moral virtue nor human purpose. The distinction between man and animal is barely tenable. What it means to be properly human is effectively inconceivable. In Arendt's view the loss entailed in this view for both politics and philosophy is substantial. Not only did the *vita contemplativa* become an "altogether meaningless"[29] activity, the *vita activa* itself suffered greatly. In it the traditionally lowest activity of labour emerged as the highest one, since labour was now seen as serving both *biological needs* and *human aspirations*. Marx was the last, albeit the most brilliant, in a long line of modern thinkers to discover the identity of necessity and humanity in the "fertile" bed of labour.[30]

From the preceding remarks it should be apparent that Arendt's thought is unusual and original. Politics as she understands it certainly departs from the recurrent pieties of classical and modern thought. Her politics will have no truck—at least not directly—with moulding souls or ministering to the needs of the body. Both lie outside the province of politics proper: the one is metapolitical, the latter is pre-political. Both spring from impulses antithetical to politics: moral virtue in the classical tradition and natural good in the modern tradition. If the former ascended to truth beyond dispute, the latter descended into the closed reality of the body.

In view of her critical stance towards the whole tradition of political theory, it is crucial to understand that she has much in common with the classical tradition. Even though she argues against it, she never rejects the classical tradition altogether. Her critique of this tradition accepts the possibility and the need for political theorizing. In fact, her thinking on politics is beholden to the classical mediation on politics, especially to Aristotle. To miss the shared impulse animating Plato, Aristotle, and Arendt is to misunderstand the basis of her thought. Her disagreement with them lies elsewhere: on the notion of the political and what it entails.

Whatever the differences between Plato and Aristotle, they prize transcendental motif: the quest for immortalizing. They see excellence as the mainstay of *human* existence. They see human status as a transcendental norm sanctioned by something other than man himself. In other words, in this tradition to be properly human is the goal actively pursued in accordance with certain standards of excellence. And to strive for excellence is to emulate standards beyond natural man: standards invariably unattainable but no less real because of that. Under no circumstances could natural life be taken as its own justification.

Arendt shares unequivocally this transcendental impulse to excel. To be political in her sense is synonymous with the claim to excellence and human status. For Arendt, between men who share a common world it is in politics that excellence can be had. In the human condition—the condition of plurality—in which men find themselves, such excellence asserted in public is the best men can and should hope for: it is the human good. This human good is a worldly good to be distinguished from moral and natural goods, both of which are inherently unworldly. But it is a worldly good which is at the same time a transcendent good. In her own words, "no politics . . . is possible without this transcendence into a potential earthly immortality."[31] Arendt thus connects politics with transcendent excellence and human good.

To retain this transcendental impulse is to insist on the link between the realm of thought and the world of action, between the *vita contemplativa* and the *vita activa*. This is precisely what Arendt insists upon because the one makes sense only in terms of the other. To sever the link between the two is to dispense with transcendental claims in the realms of both morality and politics. And do so is to rob *human* existence of its meaning, which is exactly what happened in the modern tradition. Freed utterly from the claims of the *vita contemplativa, vita activa* became fully active: only then did "life as such, the labouring metabolism of men and nature . . . unfold in its entire fertility."[32]

In Arendt's political theory the status of *vita contemplativa* is less than fully clear. *Vita contemplativa* as contemplation has no bearing on the realm of politics; indeed it is destructive of the political realm because of its preoccupation with truth and the absolute good. In the *Life* Arendt reiterates this view with more conviction than in any of her previous writings. *Vita contemplativa*, nevertheless, has a general claim on the *vita activa* because political action is not mindless and not devoid of thought or mental skill. But Arendt never spelled out the nature and the limits of the claims of the mind on politics: she simply asserted that the *vita contemplativa* as normal thinking had to be part of the *vita activa*. This hardly comes as a surprise since the distinction she drew between the *vita contemplativa* and *vita activa* is sharp enough to prevent the *vita contemplativa* from playing a significant and material role in the *vita activa*. Hence her inability to furnish an argument supporting her assertion. Nevertheless Arendt's central point can be readily granted: that in the final analysis the *vita activa*, politics and the public realm, must be presumed to have access to thinking and thought. Thus she intended neither to subordinate *vita activa* to the *vita contemplativa* nor to entirely eliminate *vita contemplativa* from the range of ordinary political experience.

The status of the *vita contemplativa* is less problematic and fairly clear in her view of the task of political theory as distinct from that of the public realm. Though this distinction is central to her thought, Arendt did not take the trouble to make it. For the *vita contemplativa* there is no place within the turbulent public realm. By contrast, political theory depends on the *vita contemplativa* because it is obviously a species of thought and thinking. As such *vita contemplativa*, understood as thought and reason, never ceases to be binding upon the activity of political theorizing. But since the phenomena of politics are freedom and action, political theory, if it is to be political, must remain tensely sensitive to the claims of the *vita activa* as the dominant principle of relevance and exclusion. *Political* theory must follow the articulation of political life, not of intellectual, moral or natural life. In this sense political theory is consciously anti-teleological but not anti-normative. For Arendt this is fundamental, because teleological action is circumscribed action and therefore no longer action. Stated differently, politics as action is historical in the sense that it is unknown and unknowable until it happens. Thus *political theory* stakes out a narrow path between the exigent demands of *existential action* and the teleological imperatives of *political philosophy*. This is the peculiar and limited sense in which the *vita contemplativa* is an intrinsic part of the *vita activa* in Arendt's political theory.

In the context of this conception of political theory, it is evident that her critique of classical theory is strictly political, not philosophical. In Plato, for example, it is the principle of restraint and self-mastery that lies at the centre of politics. This is a view of politics exclusively as art, as moral order. In contrast, Arendt's critique of modern theory is both philosophical and political. In Hobbes, for example, we witness the attempt to "get rid of metaphysics"[33] to allow the perpetual accumulation of natural possessions. The principle of life itself triumphs over and negates the possibility of politics. Market morality undermines the elementary basis of civic humanity. The modern tradition understands neither the claims of *vita contemplativa* nor those of *vita activa*.

For Arendt, politics is not politics without a principle of action: extraordinary acts which cut through the pattern of ordered behaviour. A "political" conception of politics—that is, political thought—requires simultaneous commitment to art and action as cognate principles.[34] What Arendt is after, is politics as the paradoxical *order of freedom*. Art articulates the spatial arena and action provides the (heroic) content of politics. Between the perpetual pull of philosophic truth on one side and historical novelty on the other lies the realm of politics and political theory proper. Thus political theory is not, in terms of its motivating thrust, comparable to political philosophy in the traditional sense. For Arendt, political theory is a particular way of conceptualizing the world, just as politics is a specific mode of shared existence.

What Arendt does, and understands herself to be doing, is in "manifest contradiction"[35] to "our philosophical tradition of political thought."[36] In her writings she attempts to articulate a body of political theory proper. Political facts thrown up in the course of history combine with insights threading the tradition to shape this radical quest. In line with the classical tradition her political vision is sharply normative. She knows what we ought to be doing; how men could and should live is as much part of her political passion as it was for Plato and Aristotle. Like them she is an aristocrat in temper, impatient with mediocrity and its excuses. Like them as well she displays the characteristic patrician contempt for the run of the mill.

Such is the reinterpreted status and "predicament" of the tradition in Arendt's thought. But it is a predicament which is tied to the reduced credibility and the diminished intelligibility of the tradition in the contemporary world.[37] For Arendt the origin of this predicament *and* the possibility of understanding politics anew, lies in the historical fact of the Holocaust: the totalitarian wedge driven into the heart of occidental thought and history.

THE HOLOCAUST

> Totalitarian domination . . . has broken the continuity of occidental history.[38]

In his review of *The Origins of Totalitarianism*, Eric Voegelin disagreed with Arendt's method of treating the existential phenomena of totalitarianism as identical with its essential nature. Voegelin argued that its essence could only be grasped with the aid of "a well developed philosophical anthropology;" otherwise "the emotionally existing will overshadow the essential."[39] Voegelin wished to stress the "essential sameness" of totalitarianism and similar catastrophes in the occidental past, notwithstanding the phenomenal differences between them.

By asserting the need for a "philosophical anthropology" Voegelin intended to invoke the weight of the classical tradition as crucial in evaluating this phenomenon. He argued that totalitarianism could only be understood if it was acknowledged that its doctrinal root was the heretical "immanentist sectarianism" traceable to the Middle Ages. For Voegelin, immanentism, the spiritual disease of modernity, was the anti-transcendental ground on which totalitarianism eventually flourished. Voegelin was claiming that modern totalitarianism was not new in essence because totalitarian practice was foreshadowed in the rise of the immanentist movement and came to "fruition" in the twentieth century.[40] For Voegelin, modern totalitarianism was not unexpected since the immanentist attack on the classical tradition of Greek and Christian transcendence. Once the notion of spiritual limits had lost ground, what came to pass was a matter of time.

Voegelin was both right and wrong. He was right to see that Arendt insisted on the essential novelty of totalitarianism. But he was wrong in arguing that Arendt derived the essential nature of totalitarianism *purely* in terms of the phenomenal evidence embedded in it. There was more to her analysis than that. As we consider her view of totalitarianism the substantial difference between Voegelin's and Arendt's attitude to the classical tradition will also become apparent.

Arendt sees the "event of totalitarian domination itself" as extraordinary. Nothing like it had ever occurred, even if close parallels could be found in the occidental past. The event itself was unprecedented in the most exacting sense of the word. But while its unprecedentedness was unarguable on the level of phenomenal differences, it was not exhausted by it. For Arendt, the unprecedentedness of totalitarianism had also to do with the intimately related fact that

its considered policies have exploded our traditional categories of political thought (totalitarian domination is unlike all forms of tyranny and despotism we know of) and the standards of our moral judgement (totalitarian crimes are very inadequately described as "murder" and totalitarian criminals can hardly be punished as "murderers").[41]

Totalitarian domination was unique, but unique in such a spectacularly immoral way that it made intelligibility impossible. The grotesquely inhuman character of the event defied even the outer reaches of human credulity. Voegelin took this to mean that Arendt was arguing the essential and "positive" continuity of occidental practice until this event and he was rightly dubious about her claim. In fact, Arendt's thesis centred, not on the substantive continuity of occidental history as such, but on the intellectual and moral continuity of our capacity to *understand* historical practice prior to this event. In other words, totalitarianism constitutes an unprecedented event in the stream of occidental practice because it ruptured "all our traditions" of thought and judgement.[42] Consequently, according to Arendt the extant "theoretical instruments" are not just pitifully inadequate (as in Voegelin's view) but irrelevant: the event had shattered the universe of meaningful moral and political discourse. Indeed, Arendt's thesis about totalitarianism is not fully intelligible unless this event is understood as an unprecedented assault on the hallowed categories of Western metaphysics: totalitarianism "has usurped the dignity of our tradition."[43]

For Arendt the nature of totalitarian domination largely undermined the validity of classical political judgement. Totalitarianism introduced practices in political life which were not anticipated in the most morbid speculations of classical thinkers on civic perversion. In Voegelin's view, on the other hand, totalitarianism was the direct result of the modern denial of classical transcendentalism: it fed on "the spiritual disease of agnosticism [which] is the peculiar problem of modern masses."[44] For him, totalitarianism represented no more than another departure—albeit an extremely foul one[45]—from the classical wisdom on politics. Unlike Arendt's, Voegelin's faith in the absolute validity of the classical tradition has remained intact.

For Arendt there is another sense in which the event of totalitarianism marks a hiatus in occidental political practice, a sense so basic to human existence that it left a permanent scar on Arendt's moral sensibility and profoundly influenced her approach to politics. In her view none of the recorded events in the history of Western man prior to the Holocaust ever ruptured the human structures of *reality*.[46] She means not just the particular reality of a specific period or time but the sense and structure of reality as such. This notion of reality recurs in her work with an almost oppressive frequency. Unless it is appreciated in all seriousness, much of what Arendt has to say about politics may seem peripheral if not outlandish.

From the outset Arendt concedes with equanimity that

through centuries the extermination of native people went hand in hand with the colonization of the Americas, Australia and Africa; slavery is one of the oldest institutions of mankind.

Not even concentration camps are an invention of totalitarian movements. They emerge for the first time during the Boer War. . . . All this clearly points to totalitarian methods of domination.[47]

In these passages Arendt appears to be reconciled and inured to the practice of violence among men. To suffer and inflict suffering is for her quite normal, she is far from condemning the exercise of violence *per se*: in fact her vision of politics presupposes the need to resort to violence and domination. For her violence is a natural and legitimate human activity but in its proper place, in the realm of necessity.[48] Hardly less important is the fact Arendt is not particularly perturbed by the numbers involved: over 25 million murdered in the Congo between 1890 and 1911, an occurrence to which she herself draws attention. To be fair, she does recognize the stark immensity of the crime, but the nature of her remarks does not suggest that she was truly shocked by it. This occurrence serves as just another instance in her "argument" that grand atrocity is more or less a settled habit among men. In view of her stand on these matters it may seem astonishing that Arendt was "moved" by the Nazi Holocaust.

For Arendt the absolute uniqueness of the Holocaust has to do with the nature of the astringent and experimental aesthetics of Nazi terror and its implications for the status of man. The bureaucratic finesse, untainted by personal pleasure, with which the Nazis disposed of undesirables is truly shocking. The "normal knowledge"[49] that these people were human beings with some claim to humane treatment was effectively suppressed.

First, there is the fact, argues Arendt, that Nazi policies were devoid of any "utilitarian motives and self-interest of the rulers."[50] Hitler was impelled by a sense of racial mission, a vision of teutonic destiny, in which temporal motives were suspect. Arendt asserts that motives, no matter how sordid or silly, have limited aims and thus retain their *human* comprehensibility because they participate in the ordinary politics and economics of reality: power and wealth. This is a crucial point: the principle of self-interest is a necessary ingredient in the construction of reality and an effective foil against the ascetic selflessness of the totalitarian mentality. In Arendt's view, while selflessness, because of its indifference to personal interest, may well be a moral virtue, it is certainly not a political virtue and may even spell doom in the human world. In human affairs, as was the case with Nazism, "moral" ideals often brook no opposition: the Jews stood in the way of Aryan preeminence and they had to die.

Secondly, the victims were treated "as if they no longer existed, as if what happened to them was no longer of interest to anybody."[51] In the privacy of the concentration camps, away from the public realm, the victims were deprived of the elementary right to be objects of human care and concern. Few relations and friends on the outside knew if those within were dead or alive. Unseen and unheard, they had ceased to exist for the world outside. The Nazis were thus able to experiment with, to consume bit by bit, the prepared bodies of their mastered victims without any trace of passion. Outside the normal realm of life and death, which need public confirmation to assure their reality, even death was deprived of its minimal dignity.

Thirdly, there was the discovery of racial origin as the criterion of natural guilt. For the Jews as the "centre of Nazi ideology"[52] life in the most basic sense became impossible within this macabre context. Whatever one did or did not do ceased to matter at all: to be Jewish (or Gypsy or Slav) was quite enough. In her own words: "under no circumstances (could) the concentration camp become a calculable punishment for definite offences."[53] Death became the automatic consequence of the accident of racial origin.

Finally, there was the shocking efficacy with which the objective difference between murders and victims was resolved into a tacit moral equality of the persecutors and the persecuted.[54] This was the horrible result of the Nazi practice of using Jewish capos, "who were more hated than the SS"[55] to "escort" their fellow Jews to their death. Guilt and innocence became mere words in the face of this "reality," as irrelevant as the distinction between fact and fantasy outside the "structure of consequence and responsibility" of normal politics.[56]

In a nutshell, men were "plunged into the darkest—and deepest abyss of primal equality, like cattle, like things that had neither soul nor body, nor even a physiognomy upon which death could stamp its seal."[57] Willing victims for the most part, these men and women marched quietly to their death. And in the manner of their torture and death lies a profound challenge to the humanist tradition in Western thought and practice. In Arendt's view the new forms of domination correspond to a new principle "completely unknown to us:" that " 'everything is possible'."[58] Implicit in this principle is the view that nothing is *a priori* forbidden even if the proposed course serves no utilitarian interest: there is no such thing as moral knowledge and therefore no sense of limits whatsoever in the human realm. Everything becomes possible when moral knowledge is itself denied. Arendt frequently laments the "monstrous immorality" of totalitarian domination because she sees the human condition in some ultimate sense as being distinctively moral in texture. Ironically, however, she refuses to see politics as moral in intention or purpose, although she accepts that moral knowledge does exist.

What is simultaneously fascinating and intensely disturbing about the scenario of horror created by the Nazis is its resonant unreality: its "fictitious topsy-turvy world."[59] It dramatizes the more or less absolute demise of politics, and hence the source of the totalitarian denial of reality. For Arendt, to put it in terms she does not use, politics is the articulation of the master or primary reality wherever men live together in an orderly fashion. Politics establishes the architectonic foundation of symbolic and practical order: it delineates the character and the limits of human relationships in the common world. In and through politics—the distinctive organization of power—men are beholden to an explicit catalogue of rights and duties, obligations and responsibilities: the "legally protected order of existence."[60] Reality and minimal stability are two sides of a structured order of common life, namely politics.

Furthermore the lineaments of the primary reality are shared by all in the widest sense of the term, irrespective of personal talent or social rank. This reality exists independently of individual volition or sanction: it is incontrovertibly there and accepted as such by those who affirm it or seek to replace it. For Arendt this is the sense in which the "consistent arbitrariness"[61] of totalitarian practice was devoid of any vestige of reality. The most telling evidence for this fact is the human inability to speak intelligibly about its "actions." What cannot be spoken about in human terms is as unreal as it is beyond the realm of politics.

Hence in an entirely contrived forum of unreality is it possible to unleash the human capacity for terror: it is politics as the shared ground of reality and stability, as the common structure of consequence and responsibility, which defines the limits of violence permissible in the human realm. Outside its parameters of restraint, brutality and violence prey indiscriminately on men, oblivious to either guilt or innocence. This view of politics has elements in common with, but not identical to, Arent's dominant conception of politics as action. It may be characterized as the realm of *ordinary politics*, which describes the conduct of human affairs within the specified boundaries of territory, law and customary morality.[62]

For Arendt, then, the absolute uniqueness of the Holocaust is contained in the parallel assaults on the public structure of "normal reality" and the personal structure of individuality and freedom. In its successful (temporary) elimination of spontaneity and difference, Nazi totalitarianism radically undermined the human status of man: "human nature as such is at stake."[63] What Arendt means is that human nature as we had come to know it was being transformed in the concentration camps. Neither political practice nor political theory in the past had anticipated the challenge to human nature evident in the methods of totalitarian terror.

The notion of reality in Arendt is intrinsically related to that of freedom: at this level politics is the affirmation and the shaping of freedom into an independent reality. Paradoxically, freedom is as much the driving impulse of politics as it is a potential threat to its reality. If politics is impossible without the factuality of human freedom, then freedom is inconceivable outside the order of *ultimate responsibility* which politics establishes. Totalitarianism is in essence not distinguished by its mere abuse of freedom — as in the case of tyranny — but by its discovery that freedom can be used to eliminate its own conditions of existence: plurality and individuality. Totalitarianism is an exercise in the liquidation of freedom and restraint and the arbitrary mastery of men.

In Arendt's amplification of her thesis on the uniqueness of totalitarianism, a serious and significant tension merits critical notice. In her own terms human plurality is violated more intensely when more people are murdered. But the absolute novelty of the Holocaust is predicated specifically on the nature of the violation of individuality. Indeed, Arendt's real concern is less with the fact of mass murder or with "the number of victims,"[64] than with the manner of murder.

In her private sentence of Eichmann, however, she condemns him to death for "not wanting to share the earth with the Jewish people and the people of a number of other nations. . . . *This is the reason and the only reason you must hang*."[65] Eichmann stands accused of participating in the genocidal attack on both human plurality and human diversity. But Arendt is well aware that "genocide was the order of the day in antiquity."[66] If, therefore, violation of human plurality is the reason for hanging Eichmann, then the absolute uniqueness of the Holocaust becomes very doubtful because human plurality has been violated more effectively in the past. While it is true that Eichmann was condemned for "what he (had) done," it is crucial to remember that he was condemned for his deeds as a member of the Nazi state and its larger responsibility for the Holocaust.

From the *Origins* . . . to *Eichmann* . . . , Arendt shifts the ground of indictment from violation of individuality to the violation of plurality as the primary crime. Obviously the two are interrelated, but they are distinct enough as far as the character of the crime in question is concerned. In this case it becomes vitally important to know how the Holocaust differs substantially from instances of genocide in the past. Bluntly stated the issue is this: the manner of totalitarian genocide may have been unique but it is arguable if it indeed was unique, bearing in mind the availability of new instruments of destruction in the twentieth century. What is beyond dispute is the identical nature of the consequences: genocide or, in Arendt's later terms, violation of human plurality. And it is in fact the consequence—mass murder—for which Eichmann and others must be punished, even as we grant that the manner of murder was undescribably heinous. As Arendt herself says "mass murders must be prosecuted because they violated the order of mankind."[67] Genocide in the past, she knows well, violated "the order of mankind" with equal ease. Why then does she insist on the absolute uniqueness of the Holocaust?

The answer lies elsewhere. The core of Arendt's thesis has to do with issues other than the factual horror of totalitarian crimes: it is about the morality of mass murder in the broad context of "culture" and "civiliza-tion."[68] Consider her views on European imperialism in Africa. When imperialist adventurers in Africa encountered and killed *"black savages"*[69] they somehow were not aware that they had committed murder. In what way could one approach, wonders Arendt, strange and alien people who seemed to have the most tenuous claim to humanity? Murder *seemed* wrong here but did not matter much, since how could one respond to human beings

without the future of a purpose and the past of an accomplishment . . . [people] who had not created a human world, a human reality and that therefore nature had remained, in all its majesty, the overwhelming reality . . . "natural" human beings who lacked the specifically human character.[70]

Ironically, Arendt goes on to *accuse* the imperialists of doing exactly what she would have expected them to do in the circumstances.

Inability to sufficiently master nature, to fabricate an artifice beyond the one naturally given, to establish public bodies—that is the combined political and human failure of the Africans. In broader and related terms the blacks testify, in Arendt's view, to a general lack of human culture and morality: people who had "escaped the reality of civilization."[71] For Arendt, although their murder is clearly *unjust*, it is somehow not *immoral*. This shocking conclusion is unequivocally transparent in her claim that "the real crime began" when Indians and Chinese were murdered: "there could be no excuse and no humanly comprehensible reason for treating Indians and Chinese as though they were not human beings."[72] In the case of the Africans no "real crime" was involved because they had renounced their humanity through their unwillingness to establish the human reality of politics. Hence humanness or human status is partly a function of politics and its common way of citizenship. The stoical point Arendt wants to make surpasses the factual one: that the right to life *per se*, let alone any other rights, is unavailable to anyone who can claim no more than "the minimum fact of [his or her] human origin."[73] The right to life itself is in jeopardy when that right is unsupported by a framework of politics. In passing it is worth noting that her view of the black predicament is drawn in part from Conrad's *Heart of Darkness*: in her hands a literary tale becomes the vehicle for making a serious philosophical assertion.

What becomes strikingly apparent in the Holocaust is the murder of eminently "civilized" victims by equally "civilized" killers. For Arendt, the issue becomes a profoundly moral one in this context when "unnatural" human beings are both reduced to and murdered as pathetically "natural" beings, as if they knew neither a history, a tradition, nor a past of human achievement. For the European Jews, unlike the Africans, were unmistakably human in her eyes. Their rights to life and citizenship were established legal facts. In a series of Laws, from the "Nuremberg Laws" down, the Nazis carefully deprived them of their basic juridical and political rights: "the condition of complete rightlessness was created before the right to live was challenged."[74] The Jews were systematically transformed from political beings into natural creatures without any legal claims. Then and only then could they be, and were, expelled literally "from humanity."[75] For Arendt it is significant that the de-politicization of European Jewry, prior to their extermination, coincided with the Nazi celebration of blood and race— "natural" sentiments *par excellence*. In the new world there were to be no citizens, only "natural" members by right of race and destiny. The Nazis perfected the worst of all polities because it attempted to "do without any *consensus iuris* whatever,"[76] and thus remained completely isolated from moral law and justice. In Nazi Germany "natural" man viciously quashed "political" man and the "human" being. In her own words, "man's 'nature' is only 'human' insofar as it opens up to man the possibility of becoming something highly unnatural, that is, a man."[77]

For Arendt, then, the moral and cultural context decisively influences her understanding of the uniqueness of the Holocaust. But only on the basis of a narrowly ethnocentric premise is her meaning apparent.[78] Hence it is difficult to resist the conclusion that the Holocaust is conceived as a path-breaking event in occidental history precisely because it constitutes an irrevocable rupture in Jewish history. But its "Jewishness" need not blind us to the fact that the Holocaust represents an authentic hiatus in human history as well. To acknowledge this fact is to begin to understand why human beings require the protection of politics and the public realm.

Hitler's attack on "human status"[79] points also to something else which was violated with equal obscenity in the laboratories of terror: moral imagination. Totalitarian domination had achieved the unimaginable and the unthinkable. Matter-of-course presumptions and assumptions about the nature of man received the rudest of shocks in the Third Reich. For Arendt the Holocaust, in this sense, proclaims the end of a major phase in the story of human life.

Yet the future still has to be imagined and embodied. Even as imagination seeks to transcend the deranged disorder, it needs the strength to imagine. Since the immediate past cannot support, and tradition cannot guide, man must encounter again his political beginning, he must discover anew its original spirit and human meaning:

The real story of the Nazi-constructed Hell is desperately needed for the future. . . . Only from this foundation, on which a new knowledge of man will rest, can our new insights, our new memories, our new deeds, take their point of departure. . . . From innocence beyond virtue and guilt beyond vice . . . *we must return to the reality of politics*.[80]

Foreshadowed here is Arendt's subsequent preoccupation with Homer and Periclean Athens. Brute fact once diabolically outran the human imagination. The new politics and the new reality must necessarily take its cue from the immemorial promise of ancient Greece.

HOMER

Arendt sees Marx, Nietzsche and Kierkegaard as thinkers who rebelled against the Western tradition and radicalized it to the extent that it was possible to do so, in face of new historical and philosophical perplexities ushered in by the modern age. All of them grappled with the question of man's "specifically human quality," but they were not able to transcend the conceptual framework of the tradition. For instance, Nietzsche and Marx, in different ways, asserted the primacy of sensuous life, in conscious opposition to the superior position of *vita contemplativa* in the Platonic tradition.

Nietzsche and Marx were moved not only to elevate what Plato had denigrated but they were forced to deny the truth of the other world.[81] Thus what they restored with one hand—sensuous life—they undermined with the other, because in denying the "real world" of Plato, Marx and Nietzsche failed to find another Absolute. Life in their thought—contrary to their intention—became a value among other values, unable to claim metaphysical support. Nietzsche's insight that "God is dead" and Marx's thesis that there is no truth beyond this world could not but result in relativism in Marx's case and nihilism in Nietzsche's. Neither of them succeeded in isolating the distinctively *human* quality of man.

In this predicament it seemed that thinking was not possible within the tradition, nor outside it. Because "tradition orders the past," omits and selects what is handed down, Marx, Nietzsche and Kierkegaard were like guides to a past which had lost all authority in the modern age.[82] Tradition thus could not reliably guide in its last stages and in Marx it came to its end. For Arendt: "this fact may be deplorable, but implicit in it is the great chance to look upon the past with eyes undistracted by any tradition."[83]

To view the past outside "any tradition" is intellectually impossible.[84] What Arendt actually attempts to do is to encounter the past *of* the classical tradition with "eyes undistracted" by the Platonic tradition: the "great chance" to look at this past was the patrimony of her teacher Martin Heidegger. In a tribute to his philosophic genius, the occasion being his eightieth birthday, she wrote:

Thinking had come to life again, the cultural treasures of the past [i.e., the pre-Socratic past] believed to be dead, are being made to speak in the course of which it turns out that, they propose things altogether different from the familiar, worn-out trivialities they had been presumed to say. There exists a teacher: one can perhaps learn to think.[85]

The past which is made to speak in her writings is that of Homer and the Athens of Pericles. In the Western imagination, Homer's tragic vision of human existence has been an enduring, if not always acknowledged, source of inspiration. Sophocles and Aeschylus availed themselves of many "slices from the great banquets of Homer."[86] Indeed their tragedies may be seen as variations on themes pioneered by Homer: suffering, joy, glory, death locked into an eternal contest in life. Seeing in Homer his great rival, Plato felt obliged to ridicule him and his conception of life. That Plato respected Homer as a great poet is clear enough. To Plato, however, Homer's irreverent attitude towards the Gods—his misrepresentation of Gods as capable of evil as well as good, his fearful descriptions of life in the other world and his conception of changing divinity—seemed to cast serious doubt upon other-worldly Justice and Truth.

In modern times, Nietzsche extolled Homer against Plato as the glorifier of life and its harsh reality. Plato he saw as the slanderer of life, motivated by the desire to escape from its reality: "Plato against Homer: (that is the whole, the complete) the genuine antagonism."[87] Even Karl Marx, theorist of the materialist interpretation of historical progress, was at pains to explain why Homer was still a source of "aesthetic pleasure" for men of his age. The ancient Greeks after all represented the "historical childhood of humanity."[88] That they should give pleasure now needed explanation. Marx was not able to provide a satisfactory explanation.

This limited roster of thinkers who variously encounter Homer gives some indication of the latter's contemporaneity. But none of these thinkers, even when they fully appreciated the genius of Homer's vision, detected in Homer a strictly political view of human existence. That is exactly what Arendt sees in Homer. She goes so far as to predicate a proper grasp of politics on an adequate understanding of Homer. Her peculiar rediscovery of Homer is tied to her analysis of totalitarianism, which led her to reject the view "that there is such a thing as one human nature established for all time."[89] In this context it is Homer to whom she appeals, in her effort to understand the nature of man and its relationship to politics.

For Arendt *human* existence requires that a universal element underlie the particularity of historical expression. Unhampered relativism and the absence of a hierarchy in knowledge and judgement preclude both human meaning and moral limits. What is necessary is to find the new ground of judgement and guidance in the realm of human affairs. Because the past of our present is a record of banality and outrage, it becomes necessary to start again with the language and the principle of the original beginning in the quest for the new politics. But since she does no more than hint at the texture of this original past, it is necessary to reconstruct it a little more fully.

For Arendt the new politics must learn from Homer. At the heart of the political matter is the complex notion of *themis*. In general *themis* is the proper way of doing things between people who wish to act in a human fashion. *Themis* is the accepted code of conduct of civilized life: it "governs" both public and private relations between family members, Gods and men, King and men and so forth. But above all and most important, "*themis* is a principle of politics."[90] *Themis* delineates the sacred space and code of common gatherings: it is the principle of public assemblies and public action. Man *qua* man *themis* is the pursuit of the characteristic human good which is a public good.[91] And it is achieved against the competing and pressing claims of family life and private interest. *Themis* does not demand that family and private interests be neglected but that they remain subsidiary to public concerns.

In Homer, the economic, the private and the social are seen as distinct from the public, which constitutes the ordering principle. Homer sees the public good as uniquely human. The public good is not the same as the common good: it is the good which heroic individuals pursue and acquire in public. In other words, the priority of the heroic impulse in Homer necessarily entails the subordination of economic life to public life. This world of Homer is an austere and demanding one but it is also an ideal world. As James Redfield has noted: "The Homeric world is a purely human world . . . *Themis* is the center of the Homer world and the arena of *themis* is what Hannah Arendt calls the 'space of appearance,' the public realm"[92] where men assert themselves in word and deed. Even in Homer this ideal of excellence is a poetic creation and has the most tenuous connection with factual reality: it is the language of aspiration, not of fact. Homer's heroes are aristocratic warriors who all have "assured private incomes."[93] Economic reality is barred at the gates of this world, so that the heroes may pursue excellence undistracted. But Periclean Athens, it is true, partially succeeded in making the arena of *themis* a "reality," if only for a short period of time. Pericles thought that the Athenian *polis* had created such a fine arena for display of immortal deeds and words that it would no longer need Homer to assure these deeds of immortality. Arendt writes as if she believes in the truth of Pericles' statement.[94]

For Arendt this brief achievement assumes a universal significance beyond its historical origin. In her interpretation, the supreme political importance of Homer and the *polis* lies precisely in their mythical status, not in the sense that the *polis* was a figment of Pericles' imagination but in the sense that Pericles articulated the dominant impulse of the *polis* "at the beginning of the end:"[95] it was an historical phenomenon but also beyond history, and therefore true for all times, especially in the "dark times" of modernity. For Arendt, then, this original past is not in any real sense an historical one, but a statement of the best political ideal. And it is not surprising that the only example of true human excellence Arendt singles out is the mythical one of Achilles. This past is the arena of objective certainty and knowledge, the storehouse of great and meaningful examples of what it means to be human. Arendt castigates the present at the altar of this neglected and profoundly political past.

In this context it is worth noting that both Arendt and Simone Weil acknowledge the centrality of the heroic and the forceful in Homer's *Iliad*. But Weil's interpretation is far removed from Arendt's. Weil's analysis of the *Iliad*,[96] written after the fall of France in 1940, is intended to show how force threatens and kills the human spirit of both the user and the victim.

Weil reads the *Iliad* as a "Poem of Force" which reveals that "there is not a single man who does not at one time or another have to bow his neck to force."[97] Yet men are such that even the strong refuse to see that they may become subject to force one day: the strong believe that they belong to a different species from the weak. Weil sees no redeeming result in the exercise of force. For her, there is "no consoling prospect of immortality,"[98] even for the aggressive heroes. She takes this to be Homer's real "message:" that in the end the tyranny of force petrifies and subjects all in turn to its cruel lash.

Arendt, well aware of the domination and force required of the heroic man, celebrates instead the domain of force. She sees in it the only "prospect of immortality" without which life would not be worth living. Even though Arendt insists on the distinction between force and violence, and politics,[99] this conclusion must stand. Were this not the case, she would hardly recommend the story of Achilles as the "paradigmatic" example of action in quest of immortal fame.[100] To assume otherwise is to misread Arendt. She knew Homer very well indeed, and she must be presumed to know the import of her choice of Achilles as the exemplary actor. Her view of true politics enjoins an acceptance of the forceful individual prepared to hurt others and "risk his life."[101] In sum, whereas Simone Weil warns of the deforming character of force, Arendt views force as intrinsic to heroic virtue. Weil upholds the Judeo-Christian injunction against the use of force in human relations. Arendt dispenses with this injunction to side with the pagan celebration of forceful heroism as she understands it. Perhaps it is to the point to note that both Simone Weil and Hannah Arendt offered their interpretation of Homer against the background of the second World War.

For Homer as for Arendt the public-political is primary, nature secondary. Homer excoriates the primitive cyclops not because they live in caves but because they have no *themis*, no politics. Likewise Arendt excoriates modernity because organized "labour and consumption"[102] have usurped the public realm. The passion for material goods has literally silenced characteristic human speech and reduced the possibility of politics and political action. In Arendt, the dominant status of action (political good) and the subsidiary status of labour (natural good) clearly bears the stamp of Homer and Periclean Athens. This distinctive past provides Arendt with the critical point of vision and judgement. Between the shapelessness of the historical present, as it were, and the philosophical tradition of political theory, Arendt discovers the adversary power and the brilliance of this unheeded slice of the past.

Arendt's *The Human Condition* is conceived as a comprehensive intellectual framework to understand and explain the character of modern society.

But its normative roots lie in her interpretation of ancient Greek thought and practice. Hence its evaluative fertility is inherently invidious in that the modern world can only with some difficulty be described even as a labourer's "world." Indeed for Arendt, it is best seen as a meaningless and mindless society of jobholders: "the last stage of the labouring society."[103] In this world even authentic labour is barely a fact of human existence.

For Arendt the glorious past indubitably stands in violent contrast to the modern passion for "natural" indulgence. And, although she usually writes as if the modern world is a disaster, more than a few rays of hope thread her writings. She is not oblivious to the human capacity to right things. For her it is a matter of looking at the world properly, and that is why she can still hope for change. In a secular age which rediscovered the faculty of action—albeit misapplied—the promise is permanently etched in the tapestry of the human condition. She is best understood as a thinker who deliberately heightens the radical disjunction between the primordial past and the present in an effort to delineate the *a priori* conditions for the new venture into politics. The promise in the mythical past provides the impulse to imagine a meaningful future in the wake of the Holocaust. Myth inspires visions of possibility as well as its elementary conditions.

Arendt's venture into political theory thus begins with the most basic of all questions, what is politics and what does it mean for men, in face of the horror of totalitarianism and the inability of the tradition to provide convincing answers. This venture is marked by a fundamental challenge to the customary pieties and idioms of traditional political theory: it is already apparent in her dominant attitude towards political matters. Arendt takes what I shall call the *external* view of man and the human condition, diametrically opposed to the *internal* view which she disdained as unreal and unpolitical. Her external view of man is the basic reason for the primacy of the public realm in her political theory.

NOTES

1 Arendt in a letter in the *New York Review of Books* (Jan. 1, 1970): 36.
2 *HC*: 222.
3 *BPF*: 146.
4 *HC*: 198.
5 Ibid.
6 *BPF*: 157.
7 *HC*: 18.
8 Ibid.: 15.
9 Ibid.: 351.

10 *HC*: 29; George McKenna makes this claim in his article on Arendt, in *The Legacy of German Refugee Intellectuals*, ed. R. Boyers (New York, 1972): 108.

11 *HC*: 197.

12 Ibid.: 24.

13 Ibid.

14 Ibid., Ch. III, especially sections 11-14.

15 *BPF*: 76.

16 *OR*: 142.

17 Ibid.: 139.

18 *REV*: 47-48.

19 Ibid.: 58.

20 *HC*: 88.

21 *BPF*: 39.

22 *REV*: 57.

23 Ibid.: 16.

24 *BPF*: 56.

25 Ibid.

26 Ibid.: 76.

27 *HC*: 278; in view of Arendt's general tendency to juxtapose thinking and acting, it is important to bear in mind that *vita activa* does not denote a thoughtless life of action.

28 *HC*: 293-294.

29 Ibid.: 265, cf. 266-268.

30 Ibid., Ch. III, sections 13 and 14.

31 Ibid.: 50.

32 Ibid.: 292.

33 *BPF*: 76.

34 Ibid.: 218, *passim*.

35 *HC*: 17.

36 *BPF*: 157.

37 Arendt, "Understanding and Politics," *Partisan Review* (July 1953): 385, *passim*.

38 *BPF*: 32.

39 *Review of Politics* (Jan. 1953): 74.

40 Ibid.

41 Ibid.: 80.

42 Arendt, "Understanding and Politics," *Partisan Review* (July 1953): 379.

43 *OR*: ix (preface).

44 *Review of Politics* (Jan. 1953): 73.

45 Ibid.: 68.

46 *OR*: 351-353.

47 Ibid.: 440.

48 In her essay *On Violence*, Arendt does say that the practice of violence is likely to breed more violence. This, however, is not intended to challenge her established view on politics and its relation to violence; cf. *VLE*: 80, 83.

49 *EIJ*: 86.

50 *OR*: 440.

51 Ibid.: 445.

52 Ibid.: 6-7.

53 Ibid.: 448.

54 Ibid.: 453.
55 Ibid.: 452.
56 Ibid.: 445.
57 Arendt, "The Image of Hell" in *Commentary* (Sept. 1946): 292.
58 *OR*: 440.
59 Ibid.: 437.
60 Ibid.: 316.
61 Ibid.: 433.
62 Ibid.: 460-462.
63 Ibid.: 456.
64 Ibid.: 458-459.
65 *EIJ*: 279 (emphasis added).
66 Ibid.: 288.
67 Ibid: 272.
68 In her controversial report on the trial of Eichmann, Hannah Arendt noted with shock that Eichmann made a clear distinction between "cultured" and "primitive" Jews. On this basis, he was opposed, not to the murder of Jews as such, but at "the idea of German Jews being murdered," that is, the cultured Jews (*EIJ*: 96). Arendt's apparent shock is quite incongruous with her lack of strong concern at the murder of "primitive" Africans. Perhaps it is not unfair to suggest that what offended Arendt was the Nazi attempt to divide a group into higher and lower orders, who were collectively a civilized and cultured people. As well, the fact that the Jews are—for all intents and purposes—a European people, may well have something to do with her moral discomfort in this context; see her remarks in an interview with French writer Roger Errera, *New York Review of Books*, Oct. 26, 1978: 18.
69 *OR*: 191 (emphasis added).
70 Ibid.: 190-192.
71 Ibid.: 190.
72 Ibid.: 206.
73 Ibid.: 455.
74 Ibid.: 296.
75 Ibid.: 297.
76 Ibid.: 462.
77 Ibid.: 455.
78 Unfortunately, the ethnocentric strain in her argument here cannot be denied, even though it is only the Negroes towards whose fate she appears to be indifferent. Equally negative sentiments about the blacks can be found in her later works as well: see *REV*: 65-66, *VLE*: 18, 19 and 96, and *CR*: 225. Her normative political theory also tacitly entails a clearly ethnocentric point of view. Her depiction of the *animal laborans* evokes much of her florid description of the blacks in Africa. Indeed, it must be allowed that the parallels between her critical portrait of the *animal laborans* and her hostile description of the blacks in Africa are too strident to be accidental. For further evidence of her ethnocentric bias, which could arguably be described as racist, see my essay, "Human Status and Politics: Hannah Arendt on the Holocaust," *Canadian Journal of Political Science* (XIII:2, June 1980): 320-323.
79 *EIJ*: 268.
80 *Commentary* (September 1946): 293.
81 *BPF*: Ch. 1.

82 Ibid.: 28.

83 Ibid.: 28-29.

84 See J. M. Cameron's convincing argument on this point, in the *New York Review of Books* (January 1, 1970): 36.

85 *New York Review of Books* (Oct. 21, 1971): 50. Nothing in her favourable comments on her other famous teacher, Karl Jaspers, is comparable with her explicit, intellectual veneration of Heidegger, patent in this article. For Arendt, as a thinker Heidegger had no equal in the twentieth century.

86 Quoted by W. Kaufmann in *Tragedy and Philosophy* (New York, 1969): 159.

87 *On the Genealogy of Morals*, ed. W. Kaufmann (New York, 1969): 154.

88 *Contribution to the Critique of Political Economy*, ed. M. Dobb (Moscow, 1970): 217.

89 *OR*: 456.

90 J. M. Redfield, "The Sense of Crisis," in *New Views on the Nature of Man*, ed. J. R. Platt (Chicago, 1965): 122.

91 Ibid.

92 Ibid.: 123.

93 Ibid.

94 *BPF*: 72.

95 *HC*: 184.

96 Simone Weil, *The Iliad or The Poem of Force* (Pendle Hill, 1956).

97 Ibid.: 11.

98 Ibid.: 4.

99 *VLE*, section 11.

100 *HC*: 173.

101 Ibid.: 172.

102 Ibid.: 113.

103 Ibid.: 294.

CHAPTER THREE

Vita activa:
Nature and politics

THE RELATIONSHIP BETWEEN nature and politics has been central to the tradition of political theory. In both the classical and the modern tradition, the concept of nature has served as the proper measure of human and political activity. For Plato and Aristotle, nature signified the order of right reason and right moral conduct; for the modern thinkers, nature articulated the hierarchy of needs and wants of human life. In the one view, nature denoted a moral ideal, in the other it sanctioned an appetitive ideal, appropriate to the realm of human affairs. In spite of the substantive differences in the two conceptions of nature, nature itself remained the normative standard of activity in the world. In both views, the practice of politics was intended, not to controvert, but to reflect and realize the design of nature.[1]

For Arendt, in contrast to the tradition, politics stands opposed to the norms implicit in the concept of nature, in either its moral or appetitive sense. This is her critical point of departure: politics as the common activity of men and as a characteristically human dimension of shared existence is *un-natural*, if not *anti-natural*. The public realm, an artificial cluster of activities, carves out its peculiar space against the pressing and unending claims of nature. Nature perpetually threatens to overrun the public realm physically as well as spiritually, because it is the incarnation of the organic spirit which is the source of bodily life, but destructive of genuine *human* life. In Arendt's political theory, the relationship between nature and politics is not complementary, but strictly antithetical.

To understand her notion of the public realm and its peculiar virtues, it is necessary first to understand her view of human nature and her thoughts on the human condition. Her conception of the public realm is rooted in her articulation of the condition in which men find themselves. The point which should be stressed here is that Arendt does not distinguish politics

---

Notes to Chapter Three appear on page 69.

and the public realm. Whereas politics is always public, whatever is public is not necessarily and always political. In fact, it can and does happen that the political realm is often public in form but not in content. This is a critical facet of her theory of the public realm. In her ideal vision, politics is public in both form and content—her political theory is not fully intelligible without this assumption.

HUMAN NATURE

The question of human nature has received enduring attention in the tradition. Because political theory seeks to articulate the conditions of a political order proper to man, discovering the nature of man has rightly been seen as the theorist's primary task. Two main questions about human nature have been repeatedly raised. First, does man have an immutable, unchanging nature which is given? Second, if man has a permanent nature, what is it actually like? Theorists in the tradition have been divided in their answers to these questions. To recount the substantive details of this complex and continuing argument is not my intention; rather it is to point to salient aspects of the debate relevant to this study.

In the classical tradition of Plato and Aristotle, the answer is clear: man has a permanent nature and it is essentially moral and rational. In this teleological conception, the end of human existence is the realization and the perfection of the nature of man. Thus, a good political order is one which allows this to happen: more than that, it must concern itself with the "right guidance" of its citizens.[2] The classical thinkers were not only decisively normative, they subscribed to what may be called the "high" view of human nature. For them, human nature and the best political order had an objective foundation, independent of human desire or human will, in nature or Natural Law:[3] "the ultimate measure of right and wrong, . . . the pattern of the good life or life according to nature."[4]

In the earlier modern tradition of Machiavelli, Hobbes and Locke, the answer is equally straightforward. Human nature is assumed to be permanent and rational, but in substantive content radically dissimilar to the classical view. For these thinkers, the nature of man is essentially selfish, appetitive and primarily concerned with self-preservation. There are no objective, universal laws binding upon men, enjoining moral restraint and rectitude. Instead, the dominant emphasis is on the individual's natural right to life and power, in competition with other men so disposed. For Hobbes and Machiavelli, this view is unquestionably true. Locke is ambivalent: Natural Law as Reason does impose limitations on individual appropriation, although it is debatable how effective Locke intended to make the counsels of moral restraint.

For these moderns, human will is the subjective source of man's nature and the arbiter of his proper end. They see reason as the instrument of natural passions and desires, independent of strict moral purpose. Right and wrong, good and bad, are more or less personal preferences linked to the necessity of survival in a hostile world. Substituting the notion of personal right over moral duty, the modern conception jettisoned the classical idea of perfection in the name of the demonstrable needs and wants of men. In short, human nature, although conceived as permanent, lacks cognitive status as objective, normative knowledge about man: Machiavelli, Hobbes and Locke take a "low" view of human nature.

In the later stage of the modern age, this traditional faith in an unchanging human nature was challenged by the discovery of the historicity of human life. Hegel's philosophy of history, which supplanted transcendental metaphysics, rested on the new insight that man creates himself in the course of historical action. For Hegel, however, it was immutable Reason which progressively revealed itself, through the medium of men, in the course of history. Marx radicalized this insight even further. Whereas Hegel had conceived human nature as the expression of Reason, Marx characterized human nature as the concentrated expression of needs and wants in different historical stages.

In Marx we encounter the carefully reasoned idea that man has no permanent nature, that man is what he does, that man makes himself in his activity. For Marx, human nature is historical through and through. In the activity of satisfying his needs, man creates and alters his nature. His nature is the result of the "objectification" of his needs—his transformation of natural material into objects which assure his needs.[5] For Marx, human nature is the product of human doing and human making. In this historical view, man progressively becomes more human, but we have no real measure for the fully human man. From neither the moral nor the political point of view is it possible to see the end-point in this process of historical becoming. In contrast, in the classical conception human nature is given, without the possibility of endless becoming. If the latter excludes unanticipated variety in human action, the former thrives on interminable change and becoming.

Arendt occupies an uneasy middle position between the classical and the historical conceptions of human nature. Uneasy, because her complex and unusual view manages to retain a firm niche in the classical camp, without denying the historical dimension of human nature. From the outset, it is imperative to understand this, particularly since her position is susceptible to the misunderstanding that she has denied that there is such a thing as human nature.[6] For her, there is a nature peculiar to man but it is quite different from postulates about human nature in the tradition.

"In both its individual psychological sense and its general philosophical sense," writes Arendt, "the problem of human nature seems unanswerable."[7] To know human nature is to be able to define it. But to define the nature of a being whose essence is freedom is an impossible task. She thinks it "highly unlikely" that man should be able to define himself as if he were a thing like a stone, because that "would be like jumping over our own shadows:"[8] it is the *free* nature of man which precludes a definition of human nature. For Arendt, identifying the recurrent properties of man in terms of his past or his anticipated future cannot and does not rule out unforeseen actions by man. Hence a definition of human nature is restricted in its truth about man, to either known human practices or moral expectation. The nature of human nature is such that this question "can be settled only within the framework of a divinely revealed answer."[9] She intends neither to assume the mantle of God, nor to argue that human nature is beyond human knowledge.

In *The Human Condition*, Arendt asserts that "nothing entitles us to assume that man has a nature or essence *in the same sense as other things*,"[10] and that "human nature *in general* (. . . does not exist)."[11] Both statements bear critical qualifications. There is no suggestion that man has no distinctive nature: indeed her political theory belies this conclusion. What she says explicitly is that a general human nature, or one identical to the nature of inanimate things, does not characterize man. In this specific sense only can we say that man has no nature unique to him. Arendt's rejection of the traditional view of human nature can be traced to her subtle analysis of totalitarianism and the nature of its crimes, which led her to doubt the notion of human nature as a known and established fact. Totalitarian domination is completely inexplicable in those terms, yet it was the work of men. Her unargued claim is that human nature is not a static, stable property. History is lined with events which cannot be explained in terms of the classical or the modern thesis about human nature in the tradition of Western thought. Totalitarian genocide is one instance, albeit the most bizarre, of this exception.

For Arendt, men are neither naturally good nor, more importantly, naturally evil. Doctrines of "original sin" in either their religious or political versions do not appeal to her. She is not filled with contempt and suspicion of man;[12] on the contrary, she has tremendous faith in man's ability to act with propriety and decency, aware as she is of the human capacity for injustice and barbarism. And it is because of her faith in men that she seeks to account for excrescences like totalitarianism in political, not religious or moral, terms. In Arendt's political theory, I want to argue, the evil that men do is not the result of their "fallen" condition or their refusal to heed the voice of God, but is due to the flawed nature of their shared public life.

To understand the nature of man is to grasp its potential instability, the "frailty of human nature."[13] Human nature has shown itself to be unreliable and it is reasonable to accept this unreliability in the sphere of human affairs. For Arendt, the nature of man is inherently and permanently unstable and unreliable. Her view of human nature is similar to that of Walter Benjamin: "a kind of half-way house between the classical idea of a fixed human nature with its psychology of humours, passions, sins and character types; and the modern idea of pure historicity, of the determining influence of the situation or environment."[14]

In her response to Voegelin's sharp attack on her apparently equivocal stance, Arendt reiterated her middle view on human nature. "Historically," she wrote, "we know of man's nature only insofar as it has existence."[15] If this is the case, then man cannot be said to have a human nature in the traditional meaning of this term. But this is clearly not her considered view. Her political theory rests on the assumption, noticed earlier, that man has a distinctive nature. Yet one may legitimately question whether her admission does not place her within the ranks of the historicists.

A few remarks on the crux of the historicist position are appropriate in this context. Emil Fackenheim has convincingly shown that the doctrine of historicity requires two fundamental assumptions in conjunction. First, that "history is qualitatively distinct from nature," that is, that human actions differ in essence from those of nature and from those actions forced upon men by nature.[16] Second, that "man is not endowed with a permanent nature capable of acting," that is, that human nature is the product of human action.[17]

Arendt accepts the first assumption as true. The distinction between nature and history is central to her theory. For her, the problem of the modern sensibility is its confusion between the natural and the historical, and on the strictly political level, the parallel confusion between the private and the public realms. History is decisively different from nature: in history men act, in Nature they are acted upon by natural forces of life beyond their control. The second assumption, however, she holds to be patently untrue. Arendt isolates action as the peculiar quality of man and man alone. This capacity to act makes man a political and historical being, but man himself is not the "product" of history. The capacity to act is not itself historical: it precedes history, it is ontological.

Her concern for history—what may be described as her Marxist underside—should not be confused with the modern interest in economic and social history. For Arendt, history is and ought to be a record of extraordinary events, removed from what Marx called natural history. For her as for Thucydides, history is strictly human and political history: a catalogue of actions unmotivated by purely social and economic necessity.[18] Her understanding of history as political history is based on her view of man as a being endowed with freedom. Political history is the history of human freedom and action.

According to Arendt, then, man is more than his history, but history is his realm of self-assertion. History does not exhaust his nature, but human nature is revealed and known in history. Arendt thus proposes a new approach to the human condition, which lies between the ontological and the historical views of man. Her conception of human nature and politics is grounded in her original analysis of the human condition.

For Arendt, human beings "no matter what they do, are always conditioned beings." They are conditioned by the presence of other men, natural occurrences and by things of human making. It must be stressed that men and things form the conditions of life, but they never determine life. In this description, human existence is a conditioned existence, in the sense also that it is a shared existence: no man can live alone, nor can he exist as a sovereign individual. To know human nature is not to know man in the abstract, but to know him in the human condition. Although the human condition of commonality and sharing arises on the basis of human nature, it "is not the same as human nature."[19] The human condition reflects aspects of human nature, but it does not embody the totality of the nature of man.

From the preceding reconstruction and analysis of Arendt's view of human nature, it should be apparent that her conception has little in common with the realm of Nature. By human nature she actually means that part of man's nature which is farthest removed from Nature itself. The fully human man strives to be as independent of Nature as he possibly can. Then and only then he can fashion the public realm and participate in it. Arendt posits an intimate connection between politics and humanity in her sense.

The tacit assumption underlying her view of man's nature is that the whole question of human nature has been misconceived in the tradition of political theory, which has uniformly sought to grasp human nature in the singular—what I earlier described as the *internal* view of man. For Arendt, on the other hand, the thesis about human nature in the realm of human affairs ought to be a thesis about *men* (not man) seen in relation to each other. Stated differently, Arendt views human nature from the outside at least as far as politics—the common life of men—is her concern. And this outside is the human condition.

THE HUMAN CONDITION

In Arendt's political theory the antithesis between nature and politics is rooted in her unique and original understanding of the human condition—the *vita activa*. But the manner in which she articulates the human condition is singularly problematic. There can be discerned no method or sustained argument in her discourse; instead one encounters a maze of assertions, declarations and distinctions. This is not to say that there is no argument here. An argument is evidently there *but she does not make it*. Hence it is necessary to elicit and construct this argument on her behalf.

The first thing that needs saying is that the fundamental activities in the *vita activa*—labour, work, action—are not related to each other in any particular order of priority *intrinsic* to the *vita activa* itself. The order of arrangement and the importance assigned to each activity depends wholly on the judgement of the theorist assessing the *vita activa*. This crucial point is obscured by Arendt. In the *vita activa*, as she postulates it, action takes precedence over work which in turn precedes labour, because she subscribes to a standard of human excellence which prizes public action, public speech and public performance above all else. The viewpoint which underlines this standard is that of the public realm and this viewpoint is also the source of her negative assessment of labour (more so) and work (less so).

To see why Arendt values action so highly, it is essential to understand the dominant characteristics of labour and work. Then it will be possible to understand her passion for the public realm and politics in the ancient sense.

Nature is the logical point of departure. Men are initially confronted by the domain of Nature, the "realm of being-forever,"[20] which exists in its unadorned majesty independent of human will and aim. The principle of Nature is that of life itself: the principle of eternal recurrence. For Arendt, Nature is immortal and without active purpose: it obeys its own cyclical logic and its mode of existence; it neither strictly sanctions nor hinders *human* purposes. Nature also does not develop, become or progress. In this context the opposed view of Karl Marx, which he shared with Darwin, is noteworthy: Nature is not self-turning within itself but constantly evolving, even "progressing," as men force it to satisfy their needs by acting upon it.[21] For Marx, Nature is an historical datum changing over time, whereas for Arendt Nature is an ahistorical circular process. Marx consequently had no difficulty in appreciating the affinity between human and natural history. To the contrary, Arendt insists on the dichotomy—not just the distinction—between natural processes and human history.

To Arendt, man is first of all a part of Nature by virtue of having a body. He is a biological creature, subject like the rest of Nature's creatures to the relentless satisfaction of bodily needs and wants: he is "bound" to the "life-process."[22] From the viewpoint of Nature, according to Arendt, man is no more than one organism among many. He is a faceless, anonymous member of the species, a body easily replaced by another body. In the teleological realm of Nature, men exist as a galaxy of bodies "imprisoned in the eternal recurrence of the life-process."[23] For Arendt, there is no question about the basic unalterability of Nature. The life-process, however modified by human intervention, does not and cannot change its nature: it remains the same as long as life continues. There is no hope of escaping "the burden of biological life."[24]

From the viewpoint of Nature, man is simply the embodiment of life. He has no history and no deeds. As part of nature man is, like animals, at one with Nature. In this realm there is only life. Death has no meaning since Nature does not and cannot be said to die. Whatever loss it sustains is rapidly replenished in the domain of Nature. Hence the terms growth and decay are inappropriate in the realm of Nature.

Natural man is the labourer *par excellence*: what Arendt calls the *animal laborans*. The principle which he serves is that of necessity. For Arendt, labour is all behaviour imposed upon men by the need to survive, to live. Indeed the whole cluster of activities which maintain life, constitute labour. *Animal laborans* is in servile bondage to necessity, to the unending claims of the body. This process has no beginning and no end. Only the death of the species would put an end to it.

That necessity is an integral facet of human life is an indisputable fact. However, Arendt is concerned that the comparative ease with which modern labour can satisfy needs has obscured the elementary reality of necessity in the life of men. Labour is in danger of no longer being understood as tied to necessity.[25] Labour, according to Arendt, is no more than the response of man to necessity. Unlike Marx, Arendt does not allow for distinction between modes of labouring: the manner in which men labour to satisfy their needs is irrelevant. Labour makes life possible; whether the labourer is a hunter or an executive is not at all important.[26] To say this is to say that a certain kind of mentality, tied to the necessary end it serves, is intrinsic to the activity of labouring. This mentality is that of the consumer who labours so that he may consume and consumes so that he may be able to labour.[27]

Animal laborans is thus defined by the nature of need and the associated activity of labouring. History is not allowed to intrude in her view of labouring. From this philological standpoint, labour is labour, and necessity is necessity, and all men appear as identical. In *On Revolution*, in part a sustained diatribe against the labouring mentality, Arendt bluntly states her view: "Insofar as we all need bread we are indeed all the same."[28] Insofar as we satisfy needs, we are labourers; no more, no less.

Because the *animal laborans* serves necessity, he does not act, indeed he cannot act. He *behaves* according to the dictates of the body. Man the labourer is a "conditioned and behaving animal,"[29] characterized by a uniformity and predictability of responses to an equally uniform and predictable set of needs and wants. In essence, he remains the same no matter how "civilized" needs, and the methods of need-satisfaction, become in the course of history. Arendt avers that nothing exceeds in urgency the needs of life: where need and necessity rule, all other pursuits appear as marginal and peripheral. Indeed, she claims that to serve life and its needs necessarily excludes genuine concern with other activities: "to labour (means) to be enslaved to necessity."[30]

Arendt maintains that necessity is intimately linked to violence. The realm of need is inherently violent in its urgency: its satisfaction cannot be long delayed if survival is on the human agenda. For this reason, the human battle to secure and assure life's necessities is normally violent and cruel. To expect otherwise is to misunderstand the nature of necessity. *Animal laborans* will necessarily resort to "primordial violence."[31] For Arendt, it is obvious that the economic battle to secure material goods of life will always be violent, harsh and brutish. Contrary to Hobbes, Arendt contends that the violence of the economic battle is not confined to the pre-political "state of nature:" it is in the nature of necessity to be violent and to evoke violent behaviour.

As a necessitous creature, *animal laborans* is essentially also a *private* creature. He is an unworldly animal, subjective in the extreme, and cares little about other people. The private condition of *animal laborans* does not change, even when he labours in the company of other labourers:

the *animal laborans* does not flee the world but is ejected from it in so far as he is imprisoned in the privacy of his own body, caught in the fulfilment of needs in which nobody can share and which nobody can fully communicate.[32]

Hence speech is unimportant to him except as a means of communicating information relevant for his economic endeavours. For the *animal laborans* speech is strictly instrumental. Unnecessary talk is wasteful: it does not contribute to his immediate need. Arendt recognizes his lack of interest in speech as the source of his antipathy to public concerns and public things.

Her *animal laborans* is not the economic man of classical liberalism: he is a decisively more primitive version of economic man, in that the latter was never exclusively economic in his concerns. Lockean man, after all, is not identical with the aggressive, power-hungry individualist in Hobbes' state of nature. Liberal economic man paid due heed to the laws of nature. Though not a particularly attractive figure, economic man was part of a pattern of social and political life removed from untamed Nature. *Animal laborans*, as Arendt paints him, is the elemental creature indistinguishable from Nature. He is crude and vulgar and moved solely by material desires, quite unlike Rousseau's noble savage. *Animal laborans* is nevertheless a naturally social being but his socialness is something he has "in common with animal life:" it is imposed upon him "by the needs of biological life."[33] The relationships *animal laborans* enters into are spawned by the necessitous nature of his activity. The violence with which he pits himself against other men in the battle for survival is not incompatible with his social nature, because this society is no more than the crude companionship of natural men.

Though Arendt fails to mention it, time is of no consequence to the *animal laborans*. Concern for time—for the past and future—is the privilege of men who are both free and conscious of their mortality. *Animal laborans* is not burdened with such awareness, since he is under the dominion of the body and its interminable needs. For him the past will be the same as the future. In darkness or light, now or later, he has to labour "driven by daily needs."[34] Labour's painfully repetitive character and its source in the life-process precludes variation in activity. Hence his future is not in any sense historical and is in fact not a future in the proper meaning of the term, since the future is the future precisely because it cannot be known with certainty. For the *animal laborans*, the "future" is a predictable and natural extension of the present: "the prescribed cycle of painful exhaustion and pleasurable regeneration."[35] For him, in fact, there is only the present: the imposing and increasing presence of the life-process itself. Since he lacks interest in time, it follows that the *animal laborans* does not bother himself about the human meaning of life. This question is irrelevant and absurd. The human condition of life itself requires labour and that is all there is to it. From this natural viewpoint, life is its own justification. On the terrain of Nature, life is indeed a "blessing" and the happiness which labour and consumption produce is inherent in the life-process. In this context, Arendt finds it odd that Bentham—one of the leading representatives of the modern age—should have conceptualized this "fundamental reality of a labouring humanity" into a theoretical ideal. There is irony indeed in the fact that the relentlessly mundane activity of labouring should have been elevated into a norm of human existence. In her words: "The right to the pursuit of his happiness is indeed undeniable as the right to life; it is even identical with it."[36]

In the human condition of labour, man does not rise above his natural environment. He is more or less identical with Nature and its claims of cyclical necessity. Man however is also capable of fabricating an artifice distinguishable from the one naturally given. In this capacity, man exists as the worker or what she calls *homo faber*.[37] The distinction between *animal laborans* and *homo faber* corresponds to the distinction between labour and work. In neither the pre-modern nor in the modern tradition of political thought has this distinction been explicitly articulated or for the same reasons that Arendt adduces to support it. In Arendt's view, this distinction was implicit in ancient Greek thought, which distinguished between the "craftsman" and the slave who laboured to satisfy necessity. She finds this distinction implicit also in the thought of John Locke, who spoke in striking terms of the "labour of our body and the work of our hands," although Locke did not make much of it.[38]

Unlike the *animal laborans*, *homo faber* is acutely aware of his specific mortality: the fact that he is certain of his eventual death. In face of this certainty, *homo faber* is motivated to make or fabricate an artificial habitat to house him during his stay on this planet: "his home on earth."[39] *Homo faber* is characterized by his ability and inclination to make things. In contrast to the *animal laborans*, who "remains the servant of nature," *homo faber* "conducts himself as the lord and master of the whole earth," free to create and destroy as he pleases.[40]

As Arendt sees him, *homo faber* is more human than the *animal laborans*, because of his consciousness of his separateness from nature. *Homo faber* knows that he is more than biological life, more than simply a natural creature: he is a mortal *individual*. In Arendt's vocabulary these are critical terms of praise. Mortality and individuality are more or less synonymous terms, in that only individuals can be mortal, never the species. And this mortality consists in the capacity "to move along a rectilinear line in a universe where everything, if it moves at all, moves in a cyclical order."[41] While *animal laborans* is tiresomely natural in his endeavours, *homo faber* is *unnatural* in his activity. The latter, in distinction from the *animal laborans*, is not given to consumption but to production of tangible objects. This is the first stage of the fundamental antithesis between nature and artifice in Arendt's theory. Where nature is ascendant biological life is primary.

Where the relationship between man and nature is not antagonistic, human necessity rules man. This insight lies at the core of Arendt's apparent indifference to European massacres of black men during the earlier years of imperialism: as we have seen, the Africans in the European perception represented an extension of Nature and as such merited neither sympathy nor respect.

Whereas *animal laborans* never transcends the subjectivity inherent in his condition of serving the immediate needs of life, *homo faber* achieves a substantial measure of objectivity: he creates an "objective" artifice from materials provided by nature. But *homo faber*, writes Arendt, can only create or make when he deliberately destroys part of Nature: "violence is present in all fabrication."[42] *Homo faber* thus creates at the expense of nature and therefore is the natural enemy of *animal laborans*, the guardian of life and nature. What *homo faber* fabricates is a durable, tangible array of artifacts and objects, literally a realm of "objectivity" beyond Nature. This realm of objects signals the beginning of a world which provides tangibility in the relations of men. More importantly, because of its "relative independence" from Nature, it articulates the common ground in which men can establish "human" relationships:

against the subjectivity of men stands the objectivity of the man-made world rather than the sublime indifference of an untouched nature. . . . Without a world between men and nature, there is eternal movement, but no objectivity.

The principle which *homo faber* serves is that of utility. Whatever he makes is intended for *use*, just as *animal laborans* produces for immediate *consumption*. For Arendt, the significant point here is that, although use and consumption "seem to overlap in certain important areas," the products of *homo faber* were meant for use.[43] This intention is implicit in the latter's desire to house life in a human world carved out of and against the cyclical motion of Nature.

Utility therefore logically implies extended usability and durability. Objects of use are meant to last by their very nature and "destruction, though unavoidable, is incidental to use but inherent in consumption."[44] For the *homo faber* to create objects for consumption is unthinkable. He fabricates precisely to shield mortal man from the consuming process of natural life. Looked at from a slightly different perspective, *homo faber* is engaged in "reification:" unlike labour, which is non-objective and leaves nothing behind, work aims to leave a world behind.[45] Things and objects are instances of "reified" nature, elements removed from nature, fashioned and installed in specific places for human use and human purposes. Arendt avers that without reification and the violence done to nature, it is not possible to create a world. From the viewpoint of Nature, it must be stressed, fabrication is destructive: it forcibly removes, injures and destroys part of Nature. Arendt here reaffirms the antithesis of nature and artifice in marginally different terms, but on a higher level, as the fundamental antagonism between life and durable world.

One crucial aspect of Arendt's understanding of *homo faber* is that his objects lend stability to human life and in the long run serve to institutionalize stability in the human world. The fabricated community of artificial things also functions as the source of reality for men in the world: objects affirm an "independent,"[46] public and tangible reality inasmuch as labour affirms a private, bodily reality. In an admirable sentence, Arendt succinctly captures the meaning of *homo faber*'s creations: "Without a world into which men are born and from which they die, there would be nothing but changeless eternal recurrence, the deathless everlastingness of the human as of all other animal species."[47]

The characteristic tendency of the *homo faber* is to prefer the public realm and public things, although he requires privacy to create or make objects. But once completed, objects need a public forum in which they can be displayed, appreciated and confirmed as objects. In this limited sense, though Arendt neglects to mention it, *homo faber* is a transcendent being removed from Nature and the subjectivity inherent in an entirely private mode of life. *Homo faber*'s need for privacy is not intrinsic to his being but a transitory requirement subordinate to his need for a public space suitable for showing his products. In contrast, the *animal laborans*, because his labour does not produce "products," has no need of a market-place.

Homo faber is a social being but his view of sociality is instrumental. He sees social relationships as an exchange between productive and creative individuals. Hence he needs speech to talk about his work, or about standards appropriate to fabrication. His speech, however, is mainly utilitarian, confined to talking about objects primarily in terms of their use or abuse. *Homo faber* judges men according to their productivity: his standard of judgement of men and things is utilitarian to the core. Labour, for example, is for him "only the means to produce the necessarily higher end . . . a use object," which in turn appears as a means for other uses.[48] *Homo faber* does not frown upon economic activity of the *animal laborans*, but his standard of judgement is not itself economic: life is a means to work.

Although the mentality of *homo faber* is quintessentially utilitarian, according to Arendt, it does not exclude care and concern for the world. For the concept of use necessarily involves a measure beyond "mere usefulness," because use-objects are judged not just in terms of function, but excellence as well: "an ugly table will fulfil the same function as a handsome one,"[49] though the latter will be the preferred one. Utility therefore entails more than durability and functional use. Use-objects, because they must appear in public, must also conform to higher standards of beauty and excellence. And these standards are worldly standards, existing independently and *outside* him. This understanding of *homo faber*'s creations is firmly rooted in Arendt's *external* view of man and his world.

In this context, it comes as no surprise to learn that Arendt is unable to muster any sympathy for the idea that fabrication, including works of art, is a matter of self-expression or self-realization. In work, *homo faber* obeys the muse of creation, not his instincts, desires, and "subjective feelings" which are internal to man and as such must remain private. His creative activity is not for psychological self-fulfilment or therapeutic self-indulgence but for the realization of objects fit for appearance in the world.[50] In this frame of judgement, most of what passes for art and craft in modern times hardly qualifies as true fabrication: it is no more than a range of private feelings made public.

Underlying this conception of *homo faber*'s mode of activity is Arendt's firm conviction that "no world could ever be created" if fabrication were not guided by "standards and universal rules."[51] Evidently the world, as she understands it, is the product of an objective measure somehow apparent in its undisputed identity to the true *homo faber*. For Arendt, the world is the result of the human capacity to translate transcendent ideals into objects. To seek to realize "feelings, wants and needs" is to make a "non-world, the product of emanation, rather than of creation."[52] Only when creation is guided by external standards can the world testify tangibly to an objective reality different in kind from the private reality to which we are all without exception condemned.

As a being conscious of mortality, time is important to *homo faber*, but in a peculiar sense. He thinks of time as the passage between the beginning and the completion of an object: time is cast in terms of the means-end scheme of knowledge. Unlike other activities, work is unique; it has "a definite beginning and a definite, predictable end."[53] *Homo faber* knows how long it takes to make different objects. He therefore does not waste time. He has a clear sense of past and future. For him, the past is a museum of achievement, the future a challenge to measure up or do better. The future will be different from the past, because *homo faber* creates on the basis of past accomplishment. This relationship of *homo faber* to time, though not discussed by Arendt, constitutes an essential part of his claim to selfhood and human dignity. *Animal laborans* can make no such claim.

The striking thing in Arendt's depiction of labour and work is the rigidity and narrowness of her description of *animal laborans* and *homo faber*.

One would be hard pressed to find anything in common between them and encounter even more difficulty in finding analogues in the real world. These ideal types will brook no intrusion in their respective strongholds nor show any interest in the outside world. Taken literally *animal laborans* and *homo faber* are non-human figures: they do not correspond to human beings as we know them from human history.

But Arendt does not want them taken literally but as portraits, part true, part fiction, of the distinct *sensibilities* which impel *animal laborans* and *homo faber*: sensibilities which threaten, in different ways, the ideal of the public realm and the primacy of action in her political theory. Through her tendentious portraits of *animal laborans* and *homo faber* she succeeds in dramatizing the basic conflict between nature and politics. This is just one instance of her literary temper.

The third player in the *vita activa* is the true prince of Arendt's political imagination. He is the actor impelled by what I shall call the *public sensibility*. His passion is action in the public realm. There is nothing lukewarm about his commitment: he risks his life for the sake of politics and he thrives on the freedom afforded by the public realm to speak and act in the company of his fellow citizens. *Animal laborans* despises action as worthless: it neither serves nor maintains biological life. *Homo faber* is equally contemptuous of action: it produces no objects and leaves no tangible trace behind. From the viewpoint of labour and work, action is an exercise in self-indulgence and showmanship, utterly useless and pointless.

In Arendt's theory the public realm depends, for its existence, on the actor and his love of action. To make sense of her rich vision of the public realm and the public sensibility, however, it is necessary to understand Arendt's critical distinction between the private and the public and the connected distinction between freedom and necessity.

THE PUBLIC AND THE PRIVATE

That privacy is the natural condition of men is a truism for Arendt: the needs and wants of the human body and the natural functions to which the body is subject are inherently private. These things are private because by their very nature they "need to be hidden." From ancient times to the modern period, they have not only been hidden, they have customarily been associated with darkness and shame.[54]

Though Arendt fails to identify it as such, this is a view of privacy as physical necessity and physical urgency. Privacy in this sense is a legitimate need imposed on men by Nature—it cannot be a matter of deliberate and significant choice. Privacy of this kind, Arendt asserts, precludes concern with anything unrelated to natural needs. Arendt also understands privacy as intellectual or moral sensibility. In this second and critical sense,[55] Arendt has no sympathy at all for privacy because this sensibility invariably and indiscriminately treats everything as an object of necessitous self-interest. In either of its senses, she regards the private and privacy as a natural burden common to all lucky enough to be born: there is nothing specifically human about it. This is a persistent theme in her theory. Jonathan Swift's passionate horror of the body is strikingly similar in spirit, although Arendt never mentions him. Swift's admiration, incidentally, for the ancients and his contempt for modernity have much in common with Arendt's thoughts on these matters.[56]

Since antiquity, natural functions and needs have been attended to in the household. According to Arendt, the "distinctive trait" of the household is privacy. Within the household there was a community, but it was a natural community "born of necessity, and necessity ruled over all activities performed in it." The ancient Greeks, not surprisingly, identified the private "sphere of life" with the household.[57]

In the realm of the household, the link between privacy and necessity is not accidental but dictated by the nature of organic life. Although Arendt concedes that family life is part of the household, even this relationship is subject to necessity and privacy: limitations "imposed on us by the needs of biological life, which are the same for the human animal as for other forms of life."[58]

Naturally, the household is the domain of *animal laborans*. Harnessed to the wheel of necessity, he looks upon Nature as the great provider of life; he seeks to master Nature to force it to yield its fruits. But since his interest is the satisfaction of necessity in its various forms, even in his triumph he remains the servant of Nature. This paradox is instructive. To be in the position of taming Nature, and yet to return to its natural fold willingly, is indicative of the primal, consuming mentality. For Arendt, this is the defining characteristic of *animal laborans*.

Since life is given in the mode of necessity, there is no escape out of this condition. But the tragedy of the *animal laborans* is that he is incapable of ever transcending the cycle of necessity and its satisfaction, and the privacy of the household. He is none other than Aristotle's natural slave. In Arendt's reading of the human condition, Marx's hope of releasing the *animal laborans* from servitude to Nature is doomed to failure. The multitude of "the poor and downtrodden" whom Marx sought to rescue, and whom "every century before had hidden in darkness and shame," was necessitous in nature: it did not and could not know anything beyond the impulse of need.[59] To Arendt the poor are no more than poor, without mind and soul.

In Marx's historical view, the poverty and the necessitous condition of the poor were not natural but political facts. Marx did not think that necessity was inherently inimical to freedom. For him, as Arendt points out, "freedom and poverty were incompatible"[60] within a community, indeed within the ranks of mankind. Marx's conclusion was founded on his discovery that the poor lacked freedom, not because of any flaw in their nature, but as a result of their masters' control of their means of labour. In short, for Marx, poverty of the many was not essential to maintain freedom for the few. All could be free and reasonably prosperous at the same time.

Arendt's disagreement with Marx is a profound one. For her, on the contrary, the necessity in biological life is fundamentally opposed to freedom. *Animal laborans* is a creature devoted entirely to consumption as a way of life. He is a "destructive, devouring" animal hostile to anything which he cannot convert into an article of consumption.[61] The frequency with which Arendt uses biological terms to describe *animal laborans* is deliberate. Underlying her description of the *animal laborans* is her deep-seated fear of his mentality, based on her convinction that the labourer's passion for consumption, because it is rooted in necessity, is irresistible. Unchecked, it can undermine and pervert all other human activities into a bacchanalian festival of consumption.[62]

As Arendt sees it, the *animal laborans* is a fixed type, not subject to change, and necessity is a natural, ahistorical fact of life. For this reason, the *animals laborans* is a subjective, private creature, hostile to freedom and the public world. His attitude to Nature is accommodating and reverential; he lacks any interest in freedom to engage in pursuits other than economic. Arendt does not share Marx's faith in the ability of the poor and necessitous to enjoy freedom for its own sake. Like her high-minded predecessor Nietzsche—at least in this respect—she believes that "labour is a disgrace because existence has no value in itself."[63] Hence for Arendt, Marx's fusion of labour, freedom, and humanity is indeed an unholy trinity based on a misunderstanding of the nature of necessity:

A hundred years after Marx we know the fallacy of this reasoning; the spare time of the *animal laborans* is never spent in anything but consumption, and the more time left to him, the greedier and more craving his appetites.[64]

The *political* inadequacy of the *animal laborans* lies in the private and necessitous nature of his interests. In fact, his way of life is an "antipolitical one."[65] From the viewpoint of politics, this judgement is a crucial one. In explicit terms, Arendt is asserting the identity of the public and political: to be political is to be a public man concerned with public affairs, to be a *citizen* in the classical Greek sense. In a liberal age barely aware of the distinction between the private and the public, this view of politics is new in the paradoxical sense that it revives an ancient ideal, lost to us since the decline of the Athenian *polis*. Even Plato and Aristotle, who finally turned "against politics and against action," endorsed the realm of public affairs as essential to *human* existence.[66]

In Arendt's theory, the political status of *homo faber* is less clear because he is not trapped in the realm of privacy like *animal laborans*. The privacy required by him to create is balanced by his eventual need to show his objects in public and to the public. *Homo faber*'s public character, though limited, obviously appeals to Arendt, more so because the world as an objective artifact is his achievement.

Still, from the viewpoint of the public realm the utilitarian mentality of *homo faber* poses a serious problem. Instrumentality is the characteristic element of this mentality, in that *homo faber* makes things for use. The "means-end category" is intrinsic to *homo faber*'s conception of all things, of nature no less than of the world. But since *homo faber*'s measure is man the user, he cannot but treat his products as "a mere means for further ends."[67] The perplexity becomes transparent here. Without *homo faber*'s instrumental utilitarianism, no world could be fabricated; but these very standards, if permitted to rule the world, would necessarily result in the degradation of all things as means for further use. To allow *homo faber* to impose his standards on the world, "after its establishment," would rob the world of "intrinsic and independent value."[68]

For Arendt, the significance of this dilemma has to do with the distinction between utility and meaningfulness. Utilitarianism entails the conversion of every end into a means towards a further end. Equipped with this view, *homo faber* embroils the world of things in an interminable dance of "universal relativity."[69] Nothing can be worthwhile in itself, if it is promptly turned into a means for some other end. To Lessing's question, which Arendt quotes with relish, "And what is the use of use?" *homo faber* has no answer.[70] Even Plato, whose fondness for the means-end category is evident in his political theory, "saw immediately" that *homo faber*'s utilitarianism would perforce deprive everything of intrinsic worth.[71] In short, utilitarianism lacks a principle which would justify utility itself.

Arendt's critique of the utilitarian temperament underlines a crucial aspect of her theory of politics: the public realm becomes a reality when men engage in action for the sake of human meaning. And meaning cannot be the result of that which is done in order to satisfy necessity or utility. On the contrary, meaning, if it is to be had, can only come from action which is free *a priori*. In this sense the very idea of meaning is incompatible with activities not performed for their own sake. As she puts it, "utility established as meaning generates meaninglessness."[72] But it is by no means clear how the meaning of meaning is to be ascertained. To say as she does that "meaning . . . must be permanent and lose nothing of its character" whether or not the actor achieves it,[73] does not help much.

This lack of clarity surrounding her notion of meaning is accentuated by her assertion that to divine the true meaning of action is the task of the thoughtful spectator, not the actor himself; the philosophers, poets, and historians are privileged to unravel meaning after the event.[74] So the actor acts in pursuit of meaning but what his action means, he does not and cannot know in advance. In spite of this, Arendt maintains that politics is for the sake of meaning in shared human life. That this is a literary view of the public realm and the public sensibility precisely underscores the strangeness and the novelty of her political vision.

From the viewpoint of politics, then, *homo faber* is an uncertain ally. In the context of politics as "objective" artifact, his public status is not in doubt; within the frame of politics as meaning, he must be deemed an unpolitical being. For Arendt, this is the reason why the ancient Greeks were intent on excluding *homo faber* from politics: his "banausic mentality" would necessarily degrade things done for their own sake.[75] This conflict between creative art and public performance (fabrication and politics) cannot be unequivocally and finally resolved.[76]

In contradistinction to *animal laborans* and *homo faber*, the actor is the quintessentially public man. Filled with an unmatched passion for freedom and action for its own sake, the actor shows a "heroic contempt" for mere life and its necessities.[77] In Arendt's description, the actor has shed the innate privacy of his "natural" condition, to venture forth in pursuit of meaning in the public realm. Action, founded on freedom, is a public manifestation: the actor is the true public man since the "faculty of action" is what makes man "a political being."[78] This resurrected and redefined Aristotelian theme figures prominently in Arendt's theory.

Contempt for natural privacy is only the first act, so to speak, in the drama of politics: it makes politics possible, but it is not yet politics. To be a public man, the actor must strive to "be seen and heard by everybody," to acquire "the widest possible publicity."[79] In the absence of such publicity, the actor has not transcended privacy. Both the actor and his action can combat "the natural ruin of time,"[80] if and only if the actor appears in the public realm. In public action the actor rescues the passage of time from oblivion and endows it with "meaning:" time becomes history in the public realm. As Arendt defines it, this kind of publicity is outside the range of *animal laborans* and only intermittently available to *homo faber* and, consequently, neither of them can lay claim to the sense of "reality" and the sense of human achievement that comes from public action.[81]

Arendt attaches peculiar significance to publicity because of its capacity to offer public confirmation to the actions and doings of men. Without it, action would be doomed, like the necessitous behaviour of *animal laborans*, to the irrelevance of all activities deprived of the light of the public realm. *Animal laborans*, trapped in "the cyclical movement of nature's household,"[82] has no choice but to accept the resulting obscurity. To Arendt biological life only attests to the reality of physical urges, nothing more. In view of its private nature, it can never attain a worldly or historical reality, just as "to be prosperous had no reality in the Greek *polis*."[83] Not that there were no rich men in the *polis*, but that wealth *per se* had no meaning in the estimate of the ancient Greeks and therefore had no reality. Similarly, *animal laborans* has no reality because he does no more than assure biological life: nothing that he does invites or merits the publicity of the public realm.

In Arendt's view, strictly speaking, only the actor participates in a "common world"[84] which is exclusively a public world. The distinguishing mark of this world is that it is peopled by free men, sharing nothing but their common love for freedom and public action, unencumbered by private interests or needs. No one here is moved by mundane concerns, inimical to the realm of public affairs. Furthermore, no one here is of the same mind on all issues. Conflicting opinions are the mainstay of the common world. What they are all agreed upon however is the importance of this world and public action. This is the third main element in Arendt's theory: public men sharing the common world through public action. The actor is the distinctively political figure in the gallery of the human condition: a public man, jealous of freedom and the world, and acting for the sake of action itself.

Her distinction between the private and the public is radically important. There can be little doubt that politics of any stripe would be inconceivable without public-spirited men. But it is not at all certain that the demands of physical necessity are so intense as to forever condemn *animal laborans* to the senseless privacy of the "household." While it is hard to deny the legitimacy of the opposition between the public and the private, it is less difficult to accuse her of abusing this distinction: the purpose of her public realm is so relentlessly literary and dramatic that she is forced to dismiss the poor, preoccupied with the serious business of food and shelter, as barely human. But it is not obvious why *animal laborans* and *homo faber* cannot achieve a modicum of humanity in their lives outside the public realm.

In her defence, it should be stressed that what she really abhors is privacy as intellectual or moral sensibility, not the labourer as such. This sensibility is not the monopoly of *animal laborans*; it can and does manifest itself in all classes of society. Though Arendt does not say so, the notion of privacy as moral disposition accurately describes the bourgeois sensibility at its worst. To severely restrict its rule is to ensure that shared life will be human to some degree. In this sense, Arendt's attack on privacy is entirely justified. The public and the private realms can only thrive in opposition to each other.

NECESSITY AND VIOLENCE

Arendt's political theory presupposes the antithesis of nature and politics and of the private and the public. A similar antagonism defines the relationship between necessity and freedom in her theory. In substance and disposition, this antagonism closely resembles the opposition between nature (private) and politics (public).

Violence or, more exactly, the inevitability of violence is at the root of the antagonism between freedom and necessity. Public life, according to Arendt, is the "good life" (Aristotle) and it is based on violence and domination. To dispense with violence is to abandon not only politics in her sense, but also to relinquish any claim to human status. Her view on this matter is quite clear—an instance of her shocking classical "realism." Necessity is the elemental condition of all life. Life's little pleasures that follow upon the satisfaction of need and the pain involved in sustaining life are both rooted in necessity. In Arendt's words: "Necessity and life are so intimately related that life itself is threatened when necessity is altogether eliminated."[85] No one is absolved from the claims of necessity: everyone is obligated, on pain of death, to do battle with Nature. But necessity is unending and mere life itself, she asserts, is futile. If then all men attend to their needs and do no more, mankind will be locked into a collective life of futility. Such life would be an utterly "weightless" achievement.[86]

There is however much more to men than their necessitous condition. Men are blessed with the faculties of action and freedom and an "innate 'repugnance to futility'."[87] Presumably this is true of all of mankind, though Arendt does not say whether or not this is the case. To actualize freedom and exercise the capacity for freedom, she reasons, some men must force other men to labour for them, to compel them by violence: "Because all human beings are subject to necessity, they are entitled to violence towards others."[88] For Arendt the point is that domination of other men can only be accomplished through violence. The individual battle with necessity is itself characterized by "primordial violence"[89] and it follows that mastering necessity by domination of men should be violent as well.

The ancient Greeks understood clearly that the good life, political or moral, "rests on the domination of necessity" which meant "doing violence" to others. This was the only way in which some men could hold necessity at bay. Hence the Greek citizen was not only not a slave, but had to own and rule slaves who ministered to his needs.[90] Slavery was not an instrument of profit, but the foundation of the citizen's freedom.

Arendt is entirely persuaded that in the realm of necessity, violence is natural and to be expected as a matter of course. Labour which cares for necessity is itself violent and silent: its silence is characteristic of all private activities tuned to the rhythms of the body. The violence of the labour process, she contends, has to do with the irrational nature of necessity. In its urgency and nakedness, necessity harbours a "momentum" of its own, hostile to the rules of reason and moderation.[91] Hence to hope for reason and restraint in the realm of necessity is not only naive but dangerous. The danger lies in the natural tendency of necessitous concern to overrun its own boundaries and invade the realm of freedom. Using reason to regulate what is inherently irrational, Arendt seems to be saying, will in the end only succeed in easing the passage of necessity but at the expense of other activities.

On this question, Arendt's debt to the classical Greek sensibility is transparent, once again, in her strident displeasure with the intellectual passions of the modern age. For the program of the European Enlightenment, as she sees it, to liberate the common man from the rule of necessity, she has only unkind words. In her mind, there is and there can be no question of a rational mastery of necessity: the human condition of necessity will not permit it. Nor can there be any question, contrary to Marx, of palliating and placating necessity to such an extent that it no longer commands our urgent and instant attention.

For Arendt the nature of necessity cannot be altered. Necessity will retain its driving force, no matter how palatable human ingenuity succeeds in making it. Indeed, the modern age eloquently testifies to enviable success in this field. But the fact remains that it is still necessity: "the bonds of necessity need not be of iron, they can be made of silk."[92] It is worth noting that Marx would not have disputed this claim. In one of his earlier writings, he spoke contemptuously of the bourgeois practice of deepening the worker's dependence on necessity, by "enticing" him with new products necessary for him.[93] The problem for Marx was not the new products themselves, but the capitalist ownership of these objects, which served to accentuate the worker's dependence on the capitalist.

Arendt sees the problem in entirely different terms. For her, the modern attempt in general, and the Marxian enterprise in particular, to rationally master necessity was inspired not by the ideal of freedom but by the quest for "abundance and endless consumption," that is, "the ideals of the poor;"[94] the principle underlying the modern mastery of necessity was itself necessitous to the core. According to her, such mastery which seeks to liberate the poor from their misery cannot lead to freedom because, while freedom requires more or less absolute mastery of necessity, it cannot be based on *universal* domination of necessity and still remain freedom. Arendt declines to argue and defend her position. Instead she asserts that

Man cannot be free if he does not know that he is subject to necessity, because his freedom is always won in his never wholly successful attempt to liberate himself from necessity.[95]

To put it bluntly: the poor and needy must remain in their miserable condition as a reminder to free men of what awaits them should they relinquish or lose their freedom.

Freedom and necessity are dichotomous realms, intractably opposed to each other, just as nature is opposed to politics and the private to the public. Freedom is a possibility against the claims of necessity. This and other oppositions in Arendt's theory are parasitic upon the ancient Greek understanding which she considers to be far superior to ours. To them necessity was a "pre-political phenomenon, characteristic of the household organization."[96] Entry into the *polis* or the public realm was predicated on mastership of necessity. The ancient Greeks felt that violence and domination were entirely "justified" in the fight against necessity. In the household, consequently, there was no such thing as law or justice. The household head—that is, the master—ruled to suit his personal whims: the household was the domain of arbitrary violence and the "center of the strictest inequality."[97]

In Arendt's eyes, freedom and poverty are quite compatible, indeed essential for politics. She would have us understand the "old and terrible truth, that only violence and rule over others could make some men free,"[98] though she does not deny the "violent injustice" of this practice.[99] From her viewpoint, this is the indisputable point of departure for men who wish to do more than orbit in the purposeless cycle of necessity. Her classical realism even leads her to decry the emancipation of women from the fetters of the household.[100] The female of the species is a resplendent embodiment of the natural and fertile force of life. For this reason, according to Arendt, the female since antiquity has been confined to the household, hidden from the public realm: the biological force is felt far more intensely in the female than in the male of the species, although both are subject to necessity. The modern age changed all that: it released women and labourers from the privacy of the home. This event indicates with unmatched clarity the spirit of an age "which no longer believes that bodily functions and material concerns should be hidden."[101]

Her critical judgement on women must be understood in the context of the nature of necessity in the human condition. She does not think it was an accidental feature of ancient Greek life that "women and slaves" were seen as belonging in the "same category."[102] Both were under the rule of nature, that is, incapable of choosing or acting otherwise. Implicit in her theory is the claim that most women are naturally unable to transcend their laborious and routine condition. In this sense, the woman is the pure symbol of the life-process. For men, however, necessity is naturally a lesser taskmaster. Thus when men give in to the unrelenting demands of needs and wants, they are in fact behaving like women. In this case, the difference is that most women have no choice and most men do have a choice. From the viewpoint of politics, effeminacy is destructive because it entails the renunciation of violence and freedom, in favour of the ephemeral pleasures of natural-bodily life.

Arendt contends that in the modern age the emergence of necessity as the common denominator of all activities has followed upon the actual decrease in the use of violence in human affairs.[103] And the surge of necessity into the public realm has meant a corresponding decline in freedom to engage in pursuits different from and opposed to the economic. Contrary to modern opinion, Arendt sees violence as "neither beastly nor irrational."[104] Violence is a legitimate human phenomenon and its use is entirely justified in the mastering of necessity; freedom requires violence as its foundation. To Arendt, the refusal to use violence may well be a humanitarian achievement; it is one which will not enhance the cause of human excellence.

From Arendt's perspective, human status is a transcendent norm. To be properly human men must strive to realize what is best in them, and if the pursuit of excellence entails cruelty and violence against other men, then that is unjust and unfortunate but ultimately forgivable. For Arendt, as for Nietzsche, one form or another of slavery is essential to culture, politics, and human excellence. It is this attitude which enables Arendt to write that "the life of an exploiter or slaveholder and the life of a parasite may be unjust, but they are certainly human."[105] They are human because they seek to exit from the realm of necessity into the space of human freedom. On this view, paradoxically, a human world can only arise on the basis of inhumanity: not all can be human so that there may be some who can scale the heights of human excellence. Arendt's justification of the violence of men against men derives from the primacy of politics and freedom in her thought. Violence may well be human and often rational but her justification is strictly political.

To gloss over the role of violence in politics has been a characteristic tendency in the tradition of political theory — Machiavelli and Marx are the important exceptions. Arendt's focus on violence as the handmaiden of politics simply resuscitates an age-old truth about political life. But it is nevertheless disconcerting to hear her say that some men are "entitled" to use violence over others to assure their needs and wants. The notion of being entitled to do so is appalling, coming as it does from an author familiar with the consequences of totalitarian violence and terror. No less disturbing is her rigid separation of freedom and necessity, as if these were concrete phenomena susceptible to tangible division. The way she defines freedom and necessity ensures that in her political theory their paths can never cross. Those engaged in freedom will forever lord it over others who, either through choice or circumstance, attach more importance to ministering to the various needs of the human body. What is missing here is some semblance of ethical responsibility, some sense of human solidarity. Free men, or those aspiring to public freedom, seem to be absolved from duty of any kind towards those condemned to the life of labour and work.

Though what she says is cruel and shocking, it is necessary to grasp that Arendt overplays her conceptual hand to dramatize the opposed sensibilities which impel the seekers of freedom and those attracted to the necessitous life. The point of view underlining these distinctions is that of the public realm.

NOTES

1 For example, see Leo Strauss' erudite analysis of this issue in *Natural Right and History* (Chicago, 1953).
2 Leo Strauss, "On Classical Political Philosophy," in *Plato: Totalitarian or Democrat?* ed. T. L. Thorson (Englewood Cliffs, 1963): 163.
3 Leo Strauss, *The Political Philosophy of Hobbes* (Chicago, 1963): vii, viii and 156, *passim*.
4 A. P. D'Entreves, *Natural Law* (London, 1970): 13; Plato and Aristotle spoke of Natural Justice which is more or less identical, substantively, to what D'Entreves describes as Natural Law.
5 K. Marx, *Early Writings*, ed. T. B. Bottomore (New York, 1964): 128, *passim*.
6 For instance, see N. K. O'Sullivan, "Politics, Totalitarianism and Freedom," *Political Studies*, 21 (June 1973): 183-198; Leroy Cooper, "Hannah Arendt's Political Philosophy," *Review of Politics* (Vol. 38, No. 2) (April 1976): 146.
7 *HC*: 12.
8 Ibid.
9 Ibid.: 302.

10 Ibid.: 12 (emphasis added).

11 Ibid.: 172 (emphasis added).

12 Ibid.: 189-198, *passim*.

13 Ibid.: 170.

14 This is Frederic Jameson's description of Benjamin's conception of human nature, in his essay in *The Legacy of German Refugee Intellectuals*, ed. Robert Boyers (New York, 1972): 55.

15 *Review of Politics* (Jan. 1953): 84.

16 *Metaphysics and Historicity* (Milwaukee, 1961): 26.

17 Ibid.

18 *BPF*: 59, *passim*.

19 *HC*: 11.

20 *BPF*: 42.

21 See Valentino Gerratana, "Marx and Darwin" in *New Left Review* (Nov.-Dec. 1973): 63.

22 *HC*: 33.

23 Ibid.: 43.

24 Ibid.: 103.

25 Ibid.: 105.

26 Ibid.: 86.

27 Ibid.: 110.

28 *REV*: 89.

29 *HC*: 41.

30 Ibid.: 47.

31 *REV*: 110.

32 *HC*: 102, *passim*.

33 Ibid.: 24.

34 *REV*: 41.

35 *HC*: 93.

36 Ibid.: 93.

37 Ibid.: 119.

38 Ibid.: 72.

39 Ibid.: 148.

40 Ibid.: 122, 126.

41 Ibid.: 19.

42 Ibid.: 122.

43 Ibid.: 120.

44 Ibid.: 121.

45 Ibid.: 122.

46 Ibid.

47 Ibid.: 85.

48 Ibid.: 143.

49 Ibid.: 152.

50 Ibid.: 152, 377.

51 Ibid.: 146.

52 Ibid.: 148.

53 Ibid.: 125.

54 Ibid.: 29, 65.

55 There is a third sense as well: privacy as lack of interest in the fate of fellow citizens, which is implicit in Arendt's discussion of Eichmann's conduct; see the final chapter.

56 *Gulliver's Travels*, ed. R. Quintana (New York, 1958).

57 *HC*: 27, 29.

58 Ibid.: 24.

59 *REV*: 41.

60 Ibid.: 56.

61 *HC*: 86.

62 *REV*: 106-109.

63 Nietzsche, *The Complete Works of Nietzsche*, ed. O. Levy (London, 1911), Vol. II: 4.

64 *HC*: 115.

65 Ibid.: 191.

66 Ibid.: 174.

67 Ibid.: 136, 137.

68 Ibid.: 137.

69 Ibid.: 145.

70 Ibid.: 135.

71 Ibid.: 138.

72 Ibid.: 135.

73 Ibid.

74 *BPF*: 213, 225, 262-263; *MDT*: 21; *HC*: 173.

75 *BPF*: 216; *HC*: 140.

76 *BPF*: 218.

77 Ibid.: 52.

78 *VLE*: 82.

79 *HC*: 45.

80 Ibid.: 50.

81 Ibid.: 46, 47.

82 Ibid.: 120.

83 Ibid.: 54.

84 Ibid.: 48.

85 Ibid.: 62.

86 *BPF*: 4.

87 *HC*: 102; this is Veblen's phrase.

88 Ibid.: 30.

89 *REV*: 110.

90 *BPF*: 117, 118.

91 *REV*: 106-108.

92 Ibid.: 136.

93 *Early Writings*, ed. T. B. Bottomore (New York, 1964): 168.

94 *REV*: 136.

95 *HC*: 105.

96 Ibid.: 29.

97 Ibid.: 29-32.

98 *REV*: 110.

99 *HC*: 103.

100 George Kateb is mistaken in thinking that Arendt praises the "modern liberation of women:" *Hannah Arendt: Conscience, Politics, Evil* (Oxford, 1984): 3.

101 *HC*: 64; cf. *BPF*: 187-188.
102 *HC*: 64.
103 Ibid.: 112.
104 *VLE*: 63.
105 *HC*: 156.

CHAPTER FOUR
The public realm

ARENDT'S THEORY FORMALLY defines the public realm in opposition to that which is private, natural, and removed from the common. To Arendt the *context* of politics is the public realm thus defined: the *content* of politics is the exercise of freedom in speech and action in this realm which Arendt also calls "the space of appearance." As she conceives it, the public realm cannot be specified in institutional and concrete terms. On her own account, these facets, including legislation, are pre-political in the sense that they must precede politics proper.[1] Her lack of interest in institutional problems is on a par with her refusal to see economic issues as part of politics.

In Arendt's theory, the purpose of politics is internal to itself; it requires no justification beyond itself because the practice of politics in her sense allows men to be free, lay claim to human status, and achieve unique personal identities. These virtues potentially inherent in politics are deemed by Arendt to be reason enough to prize politics above all else in the life that men commonly share. Though the purpose of politics is internal to itself, the virtues which vindicate politics are external in the sense of being virtues which men value in their relationship with one another: it is the public character of these virtues which makes them political virtues.

The conceptual narrowness of the public realm, excluding so much of the necessary and the useful from its concerns, contrasts sharply with the breadth of its substantive ambitions. Arendt is unique among political theorists in demanding from politics so little materially, and so much more humanly. The positive content of Arendt's politics is capsulated in three specific concerns: political freedom and action, the kind of citizen-actor necessary to the public realm, and the intimate link between public action and personal identity.

FREEDOM AND ACTION

Arendt's political theory, grounded in a series of antithetical distinctions between the political and non-political, is structured around the conceptual contrast between the public and the private. Furthermore, she invariably defined nearly all her key concepts in terms of other concepts, so that the concept of labour, for example, is part of the definition of the concept of necessity and vice versa; and both labour and necessity are part of the definition of slavery and so forth. The same holds true for the concepts of freedom and action.

This mutual interdefinition of key concepts is analytically problematic. The problem is one of conceptual incest: thus it makes no sense to say of an actor that he is free but has yet to act or that he is a citizen who is somehow not free in his actions or that he is a man of action who despises public debate. In the Arendtian schema which is — without explicit acknowledgement — parasitic upon the Homeric social order, to be free is to be a citizen-actor in the public realm. As a matter of fact and logic, public action is part and parcel of the definition of freedom and the free man. To doubt this would be as absurd as to say of an Homeric hero that he is honourable but not courageous.

Arendt's political theory unfolds analogically as a narrative, not analytically in the sense of a methodical analysis built upon unassailable logical foundations. The resulting loss in logical precision is the price to be paid for the genuine political and moral substance which her theory yields. This is not to suggest that Arendt's writing is, in the ordinary sense, logically inconsistent or incoherent.

Two undeniable and related facts about the human condition, plurality and natality, serve as Arendt's starting point in her theory of the public realm. By plurality Arendt means that many and different or distinct *men* inhabit the earth and by natality she means both that *new* beings are constantly born and that new birth promises new beginnings.[2] Because men are similar but not identical, they feel the need to communicate with each other, and because each man is unique in his own way he will always be capable of saying or doing something new and unexpected.[3] In these facts of human plurality and natality lie the seeds of action and freedom. While plurality is "*the* condition,"[4] it is not in itself enough to produce action and certainly not free action. For that to happen, human plurality has to be moulded into an appropriate forum — a space of appearance or a public realm where men have the permanent opportunity to engage in action in the presence of their fellow men. The public realm is the result of the encounter between man and other men, an encounter of a particular kind which Arendt describes as action and freedom: "to *be* free and to act are the same."[5]

Arendt contends that freedom in its true sense is a political phenomenon. In the main tradition of Western theory this notion of freedom as a worldly public phenomenon has rarely merited serious theoretical consideration. Instead, freedom has regularly been understood to mean either freedom of the will or inner freedom. She does not think that this is surprising: our tradition of thought is a philosophic-moral tradition and as such could not be expected to take seriously an activity which by its very nature is hostile to the logical and moral discipline of such thought. In Arendt's view the explicitly anti-political origin of the Western tradition largely accounts for its lack of interest in political freedom.

The ancient Greeks once again provide the touchstone in this matter. Historically, men of antiquity experienced freedom as a factual reality in the *polis*: the freedom "to move, to get away from home, to go out into the world and meet other people in deed and word." This was the freedom of the citizen, not of the slave who was unfree and remained the servant of "the necessities of life."[6] Liberation from necessity was, and is, the crucial condition of freedom. What is distinctive about this view is that freedom is understood as an "outer manifestation," not as an "inner feeling."[7] Freedom here is freedom precisely because it is a public phenomenon, rising above the realm of privacy and asserting itself in the world. For the ancient Greeks, according to Arendt, freedom almost exclusively meant political or public freedom; freedom as a fact of human life — irrespective of what philosophy has had to say about the concept of freedom — is felt and enjoyed beyond the limited and limiting boundaries of the individual, private self. "We first become aware of freedom or its opposite in our intercourse with others, not in the intercourse with ourselves."[8]

Freedom resides in the plural realm of the "many" and requires the presence and active participation of other men. Freedom is thus unarguably political, and it is for Arendt part of the meaning of politics that freedom is its leading concern. Yet it is this very "coincidence" of freedom and politics which all modern political thought unanimously and strenuously denies. On the contrary, to the modern mind, shaped in the crucible of economic liberalism, politics is "compatible" with freedom, "only because and insofar as it guarantees freedom *from* politics" to pursue private interests. For modern man, freedom is not only not political, it stakes its claims against the intrusion of politics and the state. In this view, politics is nevertheless considered essential to ensure security for the right to engage in activities outside the public realm.[9]

Arendt knows well the reasons which motivated modern men to doubt the identity of freedom and politics. Totalitarian governments of the recent past and the present, with their "claim to having subordinated all spheres of life to the demands of politics," cast serious doubt on any connection between politics and freedom. Indeed, political freedom has been the first casualty of all totalitarian practice. For Arendt, however, the resulting distrust of politics was based on a fundamental misunderstanding about the nature of totalitarianism: totalitarianism brutally signalled the failure of politics, and therefore of freedom, not its triumph. In fact, Arendt's urgent plea for the revival of politics in its original sense is inspired by her passion for freedom, in the wake of totalitarianism.

That freedom is primarily political was also doubted in late antiquity. In this respect, the modern view of freedom is, after all, not that new. According to Arendt, the notion of freedom as inner freedom, where freedom is the property of "man's own self," independent of the world and other men, is already present in the philosophy of Epictetus. She sees it as a significant fact that Epictetus was an emancipated slave.[10] The experience underlying theories of inner freedom is the loss of a place or home in the world. To those deprived of such a worldly home, as is the case with all slaves, freedom consists in the ability of the self to do what no one can stop him from doing. In this interpretation, freedom is a permanent and real attribute of the self, so that such a self "can be a slave in the world and still be free."[11] He can thus retain his freedom under the conditions of dictatorship and tyranny. This freedom however is not freedom at all because it lacks entirely any "interrelationship with the world:"[12] unworldly freedom contradicts the very principle and meaning of freedom.

In this context, it is especially worth noting that most schools of existentialism, Sartrean or otherwise, articulate an identical notion of freedom as inner freedom. Existentialism, because of its apparent revulsion against the tradition of systematic philosophy from Plato to Hegel, and because of its related emphasis on concrete existence—as in the thought of Heidegger and Sartre—has often been interpreted as a rather tortuous paean to political freedom. In Arendt's view, the thesis that existentialism boasts a political conception of freedom is not true and, at least in this crucial respect, Arendt is not an existentialist.[13] For all its concern for the free and historical individual, existentialism remains an anti-philosophical movement of philosophers insensitive to political as opposed to some sort of philosophical freedom. Jean-Paul Sartre and Martin Heidegger are excellent examples of genuine philosophic minds quite incapable of appreciating freedom as a worldly or political phenomenon.[14] In this sense, although Arendt does not say so, Marx's understanding of the worldly nature of freedom is far superior.[15]

According to Arendt, the modern understanding of freedom as inner freedom was not based on the experience of losing a home in the world, nor was it the result of being deprived of the freedom to participate in politics.

Modern man discovered inner freedom in fear of society's natural inclination to impose uniformity on all individual activities in the public realm. Conformity is the essence of all *social* life—that is, life dominated by necessity, utility, and relationships spawned within the family. And it was against this background that the modern concept of inner freedom began to take hold. J. S. Mill's view of liberty as the "inward domain of consciousness," over which no one else has or should have power, articulated the feeling common in educated circles in nineteenth century England about the social threat to individual freedom and individuality. This difference between the origin of the old and the new notion cannot obscure the fact that neither conception articulates a political understanding of freedom. In both, freedom is identified with the private self, and with the right of this self not to be hindered in the exercise of his liberty by the state or other members of the community.

Intrinsic to the concept of freedom as inner freedom is the emphasis on the faculty of willing (or freedom of the will). Arendt maintains that the will is not essential to freedom as a political and factual reality. Freedom of the will is *liberium arbitrium*, that is, the freedom to arbitrate, to choose, for example, between "two given things, one good, one evil." Freedom of the will is indispensable in choosing between given alternatives, in executing one's choice. But it is inimical, as Arendt puts it, to political freedom: to the freedom to begin, "to call something into being which did not exist before."[16]

The power of the will is the power to command and rule oneself and others, but its aim cannot be freedom in the worldly sense. The will can dictate particular actions among a range of possible actions, but it cannot inspire action for the sake of freedom. For Arendt, willing is a private faculty in the sense that it is by nature related to the character of each individual, not to the world: the willing self is not naturally a worldly self. The will is the instrument of achieving particular and specific goals, which individuals commonly set for themselves. Each individual will, consequently, is bound to come into conflict with other wills bent on achieving their private goals. From this two conclusions follow: that the willing self is unconcerned with the interests of others, and that the willing self is naturally inhospitable to public purposes which do not dovetail with his own ends. Hence the faculty of willing is by definition hostile to freedom for its own sake: indeed "freedom" remains outside the considerations of the will. In her own words: "The power to command, to dictate action, is not a matter of freedom but a question of strength or weakness."[17]

In this context, it should be noted that Arendt readily acknowledges that "inner freedom" is vital to thought and contemplation, but its claim to freedom is illegitimate, in that it is irrelevant in and for politics. This helps explain why the concept of political freedom is absent from "the framework of Greek philosophy" prior to Augustine.[18] For Plato and Aristotle, as we have seen, it is not politics and freedom, but the *vita contemplativa* which is the characteristic element of human existence. Only with Augustine, according to Arendt, does the proper notion of freedom as the capacity to begin make its appearance in philosophy, albeit in the context of a Christian interpretation of life. Nevertheless, Arendt insists that Augustine's concept of freedom is akin to what she takes to be political freedom, and to what the ancient Greeks as well understood by freedom.[19]

The difficulty besetting a clear understanding of freedom in the modern-secular age can thus be traced to the antipathy to politics which underlies the main thrust of both traditional political philosophy and Christian thought, which continue to command popular allegiance, however implicitly. In fact, Arendt may be taken as arguing that, just as the tradition of philosophy excluded "a great variety of authentic political experiences,"[20] the Christian tradition omitted the notion of free action, discovered and articulated by Jesus as the faculty to perform miracles, as something "within the reach of man."[21] Jesus and Augustine reveal a political understanding of freedom which is absent from the tradition of Christian thought.

Arendt finds it ironical that the modern age, which rediscovered the secular realm, produced hardly a thinker who understood the intimate connection between politics and freedom. Montesquieu is the famous exception, who distinguished philosophical from political freedom. He saw clearly, according to Arendt, that political freedom entailed the capacity to do and act in the world, in contrast to the ability to be free and will freedom in seclusion from the world. That Montesquieu was able to see freedom in political terms had mainly to do with his interest in ancient thought. Montesquieu's rediscovery of the ancient identity of freedom and politics was the consequence of his by-passing the combined influence of the Christian, traditional and modern inheritance on the subject of freedom.[22]

To Arendt freedom is the quintessential component of the public-political realm and substantively it is synonymous with action because only in action is freedom actualized as a worldly event, as distinguished from an abstract claim to freedom. But action is very "closely related" to speech, so closely in fact that without it action would not be action: action is performed "in speech."[23] Hence to be free is to act always with the aid of speech. Speechless action is contrary to action: it is either silence or violence.

In Arendt's theory the overriding importance of speech-action is rooted in her conviction that only the capacity for speech separates "us radically from all animal species."[24] This is what makes the actor the most human among his fellows. Neither *homo faber* nor *animal laborans* values without reservation "a way of life in which speech and only speech" makes sense, as in the Athenian *polis* where the main concern of the citizens was "talking with each other."[25] In the world all men share in common, speech is assigned special significance because man *qua* man is also distinguished by his capacity for speech. Arendt's point is not that man does not possess reason or logic or other critical attributes, but rather that in this commonly held world, speech is the true measure of human virtue. Obviously, intelligible speech presupposes reason and logic.

Since speech is the common property of the human species, it is necessary to emphasize that action is a form of articulate and civilized speech not inspired by urgent necessitous or utilitarian interests, and it is less concerned with what is said and more with how well or ill it is said. Arendt visualizes action as occurring *directly* between men as a kind of pure human performance:

No other human performance requires speech to the same extent as action. In all other performances speech plays a subordinate role, as a means of communication or a mere accompaniment to something that could also be achieved in silence.[26]

This comes very close to saying that human life is a series of performances and that political action is the most accomplished literary-dramatic performance. In contrast, a speechless life or a life in which speech is marginal (or instrumental) is barely human because it has tacitly renounced the company of men. For Arendt as for Aristotle, to be political is to be able to use the "power of speech."[27] For both, the human nature of politics lies in that singular interrelationship which speech enjoins upon men and which allows them to pursue excellence (Arendt) and various goods (Aristotle) in the public space. Not surprisingly, the ancient Greeks understood the public political realm as rising "directly out of acting together, the 'sharing of words and deeds'."[28] For that matter, the political stature of Achilles in Homer's description is intimately related to his superior acumen in public acting and speaking.

For Arendt, life that does not accomplish something beyond itself is indisputably pointless: hence *animal laborans* evokes her unmitigated contempt. In comparison, *homo faber* creates a durable artifice, more objective and more real than anything that labour produces. Work provides us with a tangible layer of existence, the objective, "physical, worldly in-between" which separates and relates men at the same time.[29] But this artifice of things does not become a public, political world, unless it contains "an altogether different in-between which consists of deeds and words," that is, the cluster of objects does not become a community of things, a human world, until it becomes the arena of action. Words and deeds articulate a "web of human relationships" which are no less real and objective than the tangible artifice which serves as the structured space for action.[30] Indeed it is in action—in speech and deeds—that men create the world and its quality of worldliness. Arendt maintains that nothing characteristically human achieves human significance unless and until men discuss, debate, or criticize it.

Humanness of the world is bound up with the deeds of men in it, though the possibility that such deeds will be inhuman cannot be ruled out. But constant talk about deeds and events in the world may prevent the occurrence of brutal deeds. Where this inclination and the opportunity to talk publicly about the world is absent, as was the case in Nazi Germany, calculated inhumanity against men can flourish because there is hardly any one left who can object to monstrous crimes, since all men equally suffer isolation. Voices against totalitarian barbarism did surface but they proved to be largely ineffective in the climate of individual privacy.[31] Within this context, it is equally significant that these heinous crimes were literally "unspeakable:" it is a well-known fact that most accounts of concentration camps fail to capture and convey the enormity of Nazi crimes in mere words.[32]

Since neither the human faculty nor the fact of speech is in doubt, it is crucial to understand that at issue is the manner and the mode of speech between men. As Arendt sees it, the quality of humanness and worldliness of the world depends on speech about "some worldly objective reality."[33] What this means exactly is difficult to know: Arendt does no more than frequently reiterate this view. But her use of the terms "objective" and "reality" suggests that meaningful speech is about issues related to human purposes in the normative sense of this term. Meaningful speech avoids, on the one hand, natural or utilitarian concerns and, on the other, concerns which elicit the interest of only a few persons. Objectivity and reality, it would seem, are attributes of things and issues which command the attention of men in the public realm and which men talk about because of their common human relevance.

In Arendt's view, the "human" nature of action inheres in the fact that it is inconceivable outside the realm of plurality: unlike labour and work, action is "entirely dependent upon the constant presence of others."[34] In addition action is human, because in speech, man alone of all creatures "can communicate himself and not merely something—thirst or hunger, affection or hostility or fear."[35] In action man expresses his humanity but he has to depend on other men. Paradoxically, the activity which is the most human is the least independent. Nowhere else, writes Arendt, does man "appear to be less free" than in action, "whose very essence is freedom."[36] While action is independent of crude necessity and utilitarian passion, it is not autonomous even though only in this realm can the actor assert himself as a unique individual. In spite of the individualistic and singular origin of all action, it is identical to acting with other people, never alone. To act alone is absurd: whatever else it may be, it is not action. The actor depends not on *animal laborans* or *homo faber* but on other actors, on what Arendt calls the "formality of the public, constituted by one's peers."[37] Hence action requires more than mere plurality: it depends on peers, who are not necessarily peers in intellectual rank or talent but, in the language of the ancient Greeks, liberated and free citizens. Stated differently, action pre-supposes, on the one side, the existence of unequals and, on the other, the presence of peers, equal and equally free to act in the political realm.

Arendt contends that, contrary to Rousseau's claim, men are not born equal. Men are in fact naturally and decisively unequal but they become equal in the realm of politics. The equality that men enjoy in community is a function of their citizenship, of their admission into the public, political realm. Equality is not absolute, nor is it permanent: it lasts as long as men remain citizens and participators in politics. This is the only kind of equality possible for free men in the human condition of plurality: the equality of citizens poised, so to speak, for action. Thus "equality, there-fore, far from being connected with justice, as in modern times, was the very essence of freedom"[38] in ancient Greece.

Arendt has no illusions that "injustice" is the origin of freedom and hence the condition for politics. Political equality is the "unnatural" equality bestowed upon men who have cut the urgent cord of necessity by enslaving other men. Her lack of interest in the dominant modern notion of justice—socio-economic justice—is linked to her understanding of neces-sity. Justice, as the quest for approximate material equality, is necessarily tied to life and its expanding needs. In this sense, the demand for justice is interminable since the collective needs of men are insatiable.[39] Arendt insists that politics is no place for securing material justice of this kind, even if such justice were deemed to be a desirable goal: with the ancient Greeks, Arendt believes that it is a private "household" affair, which has no place in the public realm. Politics is for the sake of the "good" life, but the satisfaction of human needs and wants cannot be even the preliminary task of politics: it is not part of the political equation in any sense. Her standards are harsher and stricter than even Aristotle's, who after all recognized material necessity as the origin, though not the end, of politics.

Freedom and action are, thus, strictly political phenomena. Freedom is "an accessory of doing and acting," not of thinking or contemplation.[40] The "gift" of action, however, harbours its own dangers for the realm of human affairs.[41] To recommend and condone action is also to accept the dangers which accompany action. On the other hand, to renounce action in favour of stability and calm is tantamount to repudiating freedom and politics. Founded on freedom, action is naturally "boundless" in two senses. Since its origin is the faculty of freedom, action can never be reliably confined. Freedom is freedom precisely because its range of possibility can never be known or contained *a priori*. As well, action cuts across boundaries because it occurs in the presence of fellow men equally capable of acting on their own. The boundlessness of action is tied to its source in freedom *and* in the consequences which ensue when other actors react to the initial action: "every action becomes a chain reaction."[42] Furthermore, action intrudes into and interrupts processes which characterize the common life of men, and deflects them from their ordinary course. As Arendt describes it, action starts its own processes as well but these processes, unlike the natural process resulting from the battle with necessity, are new and "unprecedented" in the sense that they initiate new beginnings.[43] But even the processes that actions start can easily become automatic and normal, if men cease to act. For action to retain its distinctive status, the actors must be continuously active.

Closely related to its boundlessness is the second "outstanding" characteristic of action: its "inherent unpredictability."[44] Against the tendency of action to trespass established boundaries of conduct, men have recourse to law and its presumptive stability. Law imposes limitations, however imperfectly, on the boundless consequences which flow from action. In this sense, law safeguards "political existence" in assigning responsibility to actors for their deeds.[45] But against the inherent unpredictability of action, men are *politically* helpless because actions affect, influence and inspire other actors in ways in which cannot be foreseen with any degree of certainty. While the law may contain the effects of an action by a particular individual, it is impotent in the face of further actions which the original action may lead to. Law cannot forestall or limit actions of certain kinds universally, nor can it do so prior to the occurrence of the action.[46] Law arises on the basis of precedent; action thrives on the unprecedented.

In this understanding of action, it is clear that politics depends on perpetual action and new departures, but herein lies the danger: action's unpredictability and boundlessness constantly threaten the political order, because action in pursuit of newness does not heed the counsel of restraint and moderation. Well aware of the irreversible nature of action, Arendt refuses to impose moral standards on action from outside the realm of politics.[47] Limits that she does consider important for politics and action, as we shall see in due course, arise from within the realm of human affairs. These limits, significantly enough, do not *a priori* restrain or outlaw certain kinds of actions. Instead they enable human beings to reconcile themselves with almost all actions and their consequences.

Arendt impatiently dismisses order without freedom and action in her sense as utterly worthless: if mere order is the desired end, then tyranny would be the best form of government. The primacy of action is based on her considered view that in action men can transcend the futility which plagues and burdens all life. Yet action, according to Arendt, is bedevilled by a peculiar lack of individual control, in that the actor is rarely able to realize what he intended. In "action," he acts into a realm of conflicting aims and intentions, and hence he "almost never" achieves his purpose. What the actor began as a free being and on his own initiative, he can never control.[48] For Arendt, action has an identifiable beginning but no end. This is indeed a paradox. Unlike labour and work, action alone is not forced by necessity or utility. But the freedom which underlies action evaporates in the act of action. The actor is quite incapable of concluding what he set out to do; the actor does not have the freedom to accomplish his intention. Ironically, the actor does not and cannot become the "tangible author" of any action.[49] Once he acts, the action is no longer his to direct.

In spite of this predicament, action remains the highest human expression of freedom. Indeed, it is because action is free that it produces no products or authors: the actor is free because he is *not sovereign*. For Arendt, this is the crucial point about freedom. In contrast to the prevailing wisdom on this matter in the entire tradition of political theory, she insists that freedom is "given under the condition of nonsovereignty."[50] In this tradition the identification of freedom and sovereignty "has always been taken for granted," with the result, according to Arendt, that the freedom to act has either been condemned or dismissed as a form of "necessity," because man seems unable to retain control over his activity.[51] The traditional fusion of freedom and sovereignty was based on the "pernicious" equation of freedom with free will.[52] Since free will is the internal and private property of every self, independent of worldly circumstances, a self unable to exercise sovereignty is not free: freedom here is the ability of the self to realize fully his willed aims and intentions. In this conception of freedom as sovereignty, the free man is one who either refrains from political (external) activity and withdraws into the realm of contemplation *or*, if he enters the political realm, seeks to rule and exercise mastery over other citizens.

From the viewpoint of the public realm, the former choice is irrelevant, but the intent of the latter is fundamentally anti-political, "contradictory to the very condition of plurality."[53] Rule and mastery are ideals of the household, the province of necessity, quite out of order in the public realm. True partisans of sovereignty in politics, because they abhor any kind of dependence of a free man on other men, cannot but understand freedom as free will. To minds so disposed, the language of dependence is the grammar of weakness, necessity and shame. For Arendt, it is not a fortuitous fact that, in one way or another, thinkers in the Western tradition of political theory extolled the sovereign individual—albeit as an integral member of the community—and isolated individual autonomy as the quintessential dimension of citizenship. For example, this is certainly true of Plato, Aristotle, Rousseau and Marx in spite of the real differences which separate their political theories.[54] To Arendt, it is this very identification of freedom and sovereignty in their thought which largely accounts for their lack of serious interest in the Athenian ideal of politics as free, public action.

In the framework of her analysis of the *vita activa*, Arendt finds it striking that where sovereignty is the dominant political ideal, politics has invariably been understood as the art of making or fabricating (work) as in the thought of Plato and Marx. In the *Republic*, the dominion of the philosopher-king is a prescription rooted in a manner of thinking which clearly favours making over acting in the realm of politics. Frustrated by the "haphazardness and the moral irresponsibility inherent in a plurality of agents," the philosopher-king imposes an austere order on the chaotic spectacle of action, in much the same manner in which *homo faber* moulds and shapes malleable and untutored matter into acceptable forms.[55] In this conception, men of thought and men of action have parted company for good. Indeed, politics becomes a creative and precise art: actors execute what the knowers deem right and moral.[56] Such actors are neither true actors nor free.

Marx's indisputable preference for making over acting, in politics, is evident in his view of history as made by men. Marx hoped that once men understood the human origin of history, they would some day "make" history—that is, act in the realm of human affairs—in a rational and properly human way. Entailed in this idea of deliberately making history is an explicit desire for mastery and sovereignty, and its corollary, the denial of the primacy of action in political matters. In Arendt's reading, Marx was so strongly persuaded of the superiority of making over all other activities, that he misrepresented labour—his main concern—as the creative art of work and fabrication.[57] For Arendt, because man is an acting being, history can never be "made" by men, as an object is made by a craftsman. Like Plato before him, Marx sought to escape from "the frustrations and the fragility of human action by construing it in the image of making."[58] In both instances, it is *homo faber* in disguise, not the actor, who presides over the *vita activa*. In this respect, Marx is squarely in the classical camp, even though he was far more interested in history and historical development than in politics. For, as Arendt puts it, Plato and, to a lesser degree, Aristotle "were the first to propose the handling of political matters in the mode of fabrication."[59]

Underlying the desire for sovereignty, the prejudice in favour of the will and the preference for making over acting, is a coherent and consistent attitude towards the realm of human affairs. This attitude reflects a deep-seated fear of the human freedom to act and of the corresponding uncertainty in the realm of politics. For Arendt, it is this evident antipathy to freedom and its unpredictable consequences which underlies the "degradation of politics into a means to obtain . . . 'higher'" ends, in the entire "tradition of political philosophy."[60]

The essence of freedom is that it disallows sovereignty to an individual or a group and thus makes the public realm and politics possible. Arendt stands convinced that in the realm of human affairs, "under all circumstances, sovereignty is possible only in imagination."[61] To achieve sovereignty in this realm is to succeed in establishing tyranny at the expense of human plurality, freedom, action and politics. In view of the radical novelty of this view, it cannot be put too pointedly that the inability to exercise sovereignty does not mean the absence of freedom. On the contrary: "if men wish to be free, it is precisely sovereignty they must renounce."[62]

THE PUBLIC SELF

Freedom and speech-action constitute the positive content of the public realm; indeed, they define the public realm. Conversely it is the intrinsically public nature of freedom and speech which renders them fit for the political realm. Still, a measure of ambiguity and elusiveness surrounds these matters, and it has to do with the question of the "social" and "value" content of speech-action. In Arendt's theory there is no adequate answer to this question, because it is inspired by the tradition of political thought Arendt is challenging as mistaken in some of its basic suppositions.

In this tradition, the classical no less than the modern, it is axiomatic that politics is essentially about the social and moral issues of human life. Arendt rejects this account and with it the legitimacy of the questions it has traditionally sanctioned. For these questions are part of the discourse of traditional political theory which presupposes the essential identity of the political and social, or the political and the moral, or some combination of both. Inasmuch as Arendt's theory is radically different, her political and evaluative vocabulary is distinct from the traditional one. The "social" question and similar questions cannot be adequately answered.

Having said that, the question of "content" is still legitimate on the ground of her own theory: What is the "political" content of freedom and speech-action? Since social and moral issues are debarred from it, the *raison d'être* of the public realm has to be sought elsewhere. It is to be found in the public realm itself—to be more precise, in the encounter between public-minded men in the public space. And the possibility of this encounter is predicated on the following premise in Arendt's theory: that men harbour an "innate 'repugnance to futility' "[63] which is the indisputable condition of all life. Not all men can be assumed to feel this way, nor can all who think life is futile be assumed to associate futility specifically with biological life. Nevertheless the general truth of Arendt's assertion can be easily accepted: that most men object to life's futility.

For Arendt it is their repugnance to futility which prompts men to do well *and* that doing well is a public ambition and a public claim, not a private one. (For Arendt private does not mean isolated or solitary or lacking the presence of other men: privacy surrounds all activities associated with survival and moral salvation.) In Western thought, the desire to do well has been long acknowledged as one of the paramount springs of human action. Plato described it well: "Every one of us, no matter what he does, is longing for endless fame, the incomparable glory that is theirs."[64] In this sense Arendt's point is neither original nor arresting. What is new and significant, however, is her linking of doing well and participation in the public realm. Doing well is to excel in the political arena, in the esteem of fellow men, preferably one's peers. No one can be said to have done well if he does not venture into and elicit the approval of the public in *the public realm*.[65] Hence doing well is the same as actualizing the capacity for freedom and action inherent in men.

But freedom and public excellence presuppose a space for action. For Arendt space is a human creation; without men there would be nothing more than a sprawling wilderness. A space is always between things, that is, it is always structured space. In this architectural sense, space is literally the "work" of *homo faber*: it is an "objective" space between nature and men.[66] The Athenian *polis* was precisely such a political space, according to Arendt: it offered the Athenian citizens the perpetual opportunity to act in word and deed in the presence of each other.

This space is more than a matter of a proper physical location. Slaves and barbarians in antiquity who lived together and were "capable of word and deed" did not live in this space. Such spaces do not become political spaces in the absence of a community of what I shall call *public selves*. Pericles' declaration to the Athenians, "Wherever you go, you will be a *polis*" succinctly points to the integral relationship between sensibility and politics. For Pericles as for Arendt, the political space comes into being when people live together for the purpose of practising freedom, "no matter where they happen to be."[67] The physical space itself is insufficient and marginal to politics, though far from irrelevant. Without citizen-actors propelled by the passion to excel and do well in the company of their peers, a living space which arises between men sharing life does not become political space. Stated negatively, citizens may well decide to use their common space to enlarge their wealth and "voluntarily" become "servant(s) of necessity."[68] In this case the space of action remains politically sterile.

The virtue which characterizes the public self is elementary courage — one of the ranking political virtues essential for action. For Arendt, courage is not simply the urge to experience life in all its intense variety; it is not the passion for indiscriminate adventure. On the contrary, courage is born of "vicious contempt for life and all its interests."[69] Courage is allied to the desire to become fully human in the public realm and transcend the darkness of private, everyday life. The courageous man thrives on risking his life for something more permanent than himself. If he is a coward, his foray into the public arena is even more admirable. And his courage lies not in his public venture as such, but in his decision to abandon concern for the more pressing matters of life. In alternative terms, the public self is filled with pride and the desire to be admired publicly. In the language of Hobbes, he is vainglorious.

On this account, the true public self is a pagan in the ancient Greek sense, preoccupied with his status in the eyes of his peers and the world. Arendt is well aware that Christianity and modern opinion are united in disparaging the vanity and shameless pride of her political actor. Indeed, it is against this unanimous and critical judgement that she seeks to revive and recommend the ideal of the public actor. While courage is indispensible for action, it remains aimless without an inspiring principle. The public self is characterized by fundamental courage *and* a principle of action. This principle is identical neither with private motives, nor with particular, limited goals. In her singular view, political action springs from a principle which lies outside the self and inspires the actor "from without." This principle is transcendent in the sense that it is a worldly principle. For

Arendt such a principle is honour or glory or, in ancient terms, the love of distinction and excellence.[70]

Intrinsic to such principles are two attributes which utterly separate political action from other activities. The first is freedom: unlike labour or work, political action is "not forced upon us."[71] As a corollary of its free status, political action is not limited and defined by impulses internal to the social life of all men: utility, necessity or spirituality. Labour and work confine men to a mode of life from which *homo faber* and *animal laborans* cannot stand apart as man *qua* man. Labour and work, in comparison with action, imprison men in their respective households. Second, the principle is actualized in the performance of political action itself, not in any end or product which may be the result. To Arendt it is this characteristic of action, "fully manifest"[72] in the performance, independent of the outcome, which is the root of its greatness. In action, the public self is able to achieve a representation of his own, infinitely superior to that in any other form of activity. In the Arendtian schema, it is of the utmost importance that the actor rest his claim to having done well on the actual calibre of his public performance, not on his prowess in the economic arena, his wealth or, for that matter, his racial heritage.[73] In political action, man presents himself to the world as he really is, as a member of the human species without claims to privileges and advantages extrinsic to the realm of action.

For us, it is crucial to understand that this concept of action is an explicit attack on competing notions of humanity in the totalitarian and liberal-bourgeois *Weltanschauungen*. In the Hitlerite conception, human status and political competence attach to racial origin, rather than to actual individual capacities. On the other hand, the bourgeois ethic predicates human and political achievement essentially on the range and the quality of material acquisitions. Needless to say, the capacity for action is tacitly presumed in both versions, but action is not itself the measure of achievement.

In different ways the Nazi and liberal ideologies established an irrevocable connection between the ability to do well and innate characteristics. Liberal ideology was of course not inherently racial: it was a progressive force critical of the traditional emphasis on "birth, family and heritage."[74] Liberal thinkers (and heroes) like J. S. Mill and James Mill claimed, nevertheless, that natives in the colonial possessions were far from culturally ready to appreciate or practise liberty well. In such writings as *On Liberty* and *On Representative Government*, and in the *History of British India*, both Mills subscribed to the view that their psychology and intellectual calibre rendered the colonial natives incapable of self-government or economic and political success. For Arendt it is this insidious connection between the psychological self and favoured status in modern thought which vitiates a proper understanding of humanity and politics: as long as politics and political action are understood and judged in terms of criteria extraneous to its sphere, the individual cannot establish either his humanity or his unique identity in the shared arena of politics.

This conception of political action is a difficult one to understand precisely. And the difficulty resides in Arendt's view of psychology. Specifically, she is profoundly unsympathetic to explanations of action in natural or social-psychological terms, that is, in terms of internal motives or group characteristics.[75] She describes political action as a worldly, external phenomenon. But it is also true that the authentic actor, in her description, is a particular type of person. Psychology is thus not irrelevant to her analysis of action, but it is a kind of unarticulated psychology opposed to the modern psychology of the self-contained personality separated from the world. Arendt's public self, in the language of the ancients, is *eudaimōn*: the self is "blessed" with a distinct personality, "a lasting state of being" not subject to change.[76] Furthermore, this state of being is not apparent to the political actor and it is thus absurd for him to claim attention because of his psychological uniqueness, when he is not in a position to know that. His personality is literally public property, articulated in the eyes and the minds of his fellow men. The public self is a psychological self, only in the sense that he is a worldly self: it is the psychology of the public persona, not the private being, which is relevant to political action.

Machiavelli's concept of the public-political man of action is pointedly relevant in this context. Machiavelli's relevance is inextricably tied to his unique and isolated position in the main tradition of political theory. Machiavelli's astuteness in political matters is axiomatic. No one has ever accused him of lacking political passion. Indeed the debate over the meaning and import of his political thought continues unabated. In modern scholarly writing on Machiavelli, two opposed schools of thought stand out. According to the one, Machiavelli is the representative thinker in the realistic assessment of politics: he offers his readers a remarkably clear, technically proficient and scientific account of the harsh truths of political life. Max Lerner and Ernst Cassirer may be cited as intelligent supporters of this view.[77] In the words of Cassirer: "*The Prince* is neither a moral nor an immoral book; it is simply a technical book."[78]

As far as the other school is concerned, Machiavelli is not only a self-conscious proponent of a new form of interest-politics but also an immoral and evil thinker. Leo Strauss is the ranking figure in this school. His argument is clear: Machiavelli is the "classic" teacher "of the evil way of political thinking and political acting." Strauss is not unmindful of the fact that such doctrines are neither new nor foreign to the practice of politics. For him, however, the point is that Machiavelli is the sole political "philosopher" who "proclaims openly and triumphantly a corrupting doctrine" of politics.[79]

Strauss argues that there are only two ways of political thinking: one evil, the other moral; one modern, the other ancient. In this interpretation, Machiavelli's political thought is more than modern and evil: it is a shameless attack on all that is universally good and moral in the life of men. For Strauss, this is the "true character" of Machiavelli's doctrines: he is not satisfied to argue for immoral politics, he asserts that the "pre-modern heritage" of classical moral ideals is utterly irrelevant.[80] For Strauss, then, Machiavelli is the first modern thinker and his modernity lies in his deliberate deviation from, and his disparagement of, the classical moral wisdom on politics. Machiavelli stands accused of sacrilege *not* at the bar of ancient political practice but at the altar of ancient thought on matters political. Stated differently, it is in the name of the Bible and the moral philosophy of Plato and Aristotle that Strauss indicts Machiavelli.

Arendt's view of Machiavelli and his thought is far removed from both schools of thought. In her estimation the scientific character of Machiavelli's thought is "often greatly exaggerated." On the factual level, it seems to her rather absurd to use the term scientific for Machiavelli, a century in advance of the "rise of modern science."[81] Machiavelli's method can hardly be said to be scientific in the proper sense: the undisguised normative character of his thought, noticed by many, including Strauss, casts doubt on his alleged scientific turn of mind.

On the question of Machiavelli's moral inadequacy, Arendt could not disagree more with Strauss. And her disagreement is immensely significant, in that her erudition in and intuitive sympathy for classical thought is nearly equal to that of Strauss. Machiavelli, according to Arendt, certainly appears to be unconcerned with moral judgments but he cannot and should not be read as immoral. His notorious statement that men should "learn how not to be good," does *not* mean that they should "learn how to be evil."[82] The opposite of being not good, is not being evil. Interpretations in the Straussian mould entirely miss the intent of Machiavelli. In her eyes, Machiavelli never doubted the truth of classical moral ideals or the truth of God.[83] When he recommends badness, he does not pass it off as goodness. Good and evil were notions as well known to Machiavelli as they were to Plato and Aristotle.

For Arendt the charge that Machiavelli was morally obtuse is patently false. His apparent unconcern with moral arguments was due to other reasons. Machiavelli was opposed to both the Platonic concept of the Good and the Christian concept of "absolute goodness" as being destructive of politics.[84] In Arendt's view, the Good in Plato's philosophy signifies primary concern with the contemplation of the Beautiful—the highest idea. In his *political* philosophy, however, Plato translates this concept of the Good to mean "good for," so as to make this idea applicable to the realm of human affairs and politics.[85] The idea of "good for" became the measure for evaluating all activity in this realm. This is the standard of judgement with which the philosopher returns to the turmoil in the cave of human affairs. Machiavelli, according to Arendt, saw that the new Platonic measure was a utilitarian measure quite hostile to action and politics. Machiavelli construed Plato's diluted concept of the Good as disastrous for politics: now action was to be valued for its contribution to the contemplative-moral life, not for itself. Hence Machiavelli rejected this notion of goodness.

On the other side, the Christian notion of "absolute goodness" is equally suspicious of action in that it is a moral ideal "not of this world" and hence opposed to the claims of free action in this world.[86] Arendt contends that goodness is by nature not fitted for public display, nor can it be an accessory of action in the shared world of men, because action necessarily has consequences injurious to at least some men. Her reason is that no action can be good absolutely, and the desire to be good in the public realm is detrimental to both goodness itself and to the public realm. According to Arendt, this is the meaning of Machiavelli's famous denunciation of the church: that the interference of the Church in the political realm "corrupted" both the Church and public life.[87]

Machiavelli in this view was not against the Church or Christianity but against its participation in public life. For him, Christian values and codes of conduct were appropriate "only in the private sphere of human life."[88] Arendt thinks highly of Machiavelli but her sympathy for him should not be construed as hostility towards the realm of morality. For both, it is the primacy of action and politics in their thought that leads them to insist on the distinction between the private and the public, "the individual self, . . . and the member of the community, . . . morality and politics."[89]

For Arendt, Machiavelli belongs neither in the classical nor in the modern tradition of political philosophy. He is the unprejudiced recoverer of the ancient notion of politics in the midst of a climate of thought ruled by the canons of establishment Christianity:

Machiavelli was the first to visualize the rise of a purely secular realm whose laws and principles of action were independent of the teachings of the Church in particular, and of moral standards, transcending the sphere of human affairs, in general.[90]

Machiavelli's rediscovery of the secular or the ancient pride in action marks him as a partisan of the pagan love of politics. Only Machiavelli in our tradition could have uttered those famous words: "I love my city more than my soul."[91] Even Karl Marx with his abundant contempt for religion could not have said these words, because he seriously doubted that the ancient political man could either be revived in the industrial era or that such an ideal was worth rejuvenating, founded as it was on a slave economy.

In contrast, Machiavelli, able student of ancient history and politics in an age intellectually devoted to classical learning, could and did seriously visualize the re-appearance of *zoon politikon*. For Arendt, it was this passion for the secular-political man in Machiavelli that led him to sharply criticize the self-lovers among men. In other words, it was not love for God which disturbed Machiavelli: he was bothered by those who loved God for their own self-interest. Such men could love neither God nor the world, only their private selves and its attendant interests. As Arendt puts it: "The question, as Machiavelli saw it, was not whether one loved God more than the world, but whether one was capable of loving the world more than one's own self."[92] For Machiavelli, as for Arendt, self-love is a form of slavishness, a kind of incestuous self-concern, unfit for human beings. Self-love is inimical to both the love of God and love of politics and action.[93]

From the viewpoint of politics, Machiavelli's greatness lies in his success in retrieving the ancient concept of action opposed by "all traditions, Christian and Greek, as presented, nurtured, and reinterpreted by the Church."[94] Machiavelli's concept of *virtú* recalls the Athenian notion of action with enviable insight and precision. *Virtú* is more or less identical with what Arendt has in mind when she speaks of "freedom as inherent in action."[95] In one critical respect, *virtú* differs from action: it does not have the connotation of moral neutrality, characteristic of both action (in Arendt's usage) and the Greek notion of *arête* (excellence). In contrast, Machiavelli's praise of success and glory in politics, untainted by deliberate evil, does seem to imply a sense of moral limits.

For Arendt, *virtú* thus entails moral restraint, though it is not clear how binding such restraint is or where the moral barrier begins. Arendt leaves the question unresolved. *Virtú* and action are, however, both opposed to the strictly "moral character" of Roman *virtus* and the classical virtue of Plato and Aristotle.[96] In this ethical frame, the moral nature of the consequences of action serves as the primary measure of the rightness and the appropriateness of action. For Machiavelli and Arendt, on the other hand, action is to be judged mainly in terms of the guiding principle and the actual performance of the political actor, irrespective of the consequences which follow. While virtue in the classical and Roman sense is primarily a moral concept, *virtú* and action are primarily worldly ideals.

To us this public self seems so incongruous because he is a man transposed from the radically different moral order incarnated in the epics of Homer, where man is more or less identical with his actions. His human and moral *persona* is completely revealed in his actions; he does not and cannot be presumed to have any hidden depths, virtues and vices buried in him. Hence man is always a public man.[97] This is the ancient lineage of the Arendtian actor: he is the *moral* figure from a much older form of life, even though he may appear to be immoral in terms of later statements of morality, say, Kantian or utilitarian.

The public self values freedom and action for their own sake as productive of the highest and the best in the shared lives of men. Arendt underlines the dramatic motif as central to public action, since politics is a "performing art," quite distinct from the classical and modern view of politics as a creative art.[98] For the public self "the performance is the work," in politics. In Aristotle's usage, action is *energeia* ("actuality"): it leaves nothing tangible behind, it has no "end" but itself. In action there is no distinction between the process and the end, the original aim and the outcome. Unlike labour and work, action has "nothing higher to attain than this actuality itself."[99] The end result is incidental to action.

For this reason, Arendt discerns an intimate connection between the theatre and politics. In both, it is the drama, the nature of the performance, the virtuosity of action, which is the common distinctive root: "the theatre is the political art *par excellence*."[100] Her politics is proudly theatrical, unencumbered by any guilt about the joys of acting and action for its own sake. Jean-Jacques Rousseau's passionately opposed view of the theatre and acting, as immoral and hypocritical dissimulation, serves to highlight the iconoclastic singularity of Arendt's conception of politics.[101] For Rousseau, it was the ability to will what was morally right, just and truthful, that was the essence of politics and political man. He saw politics as the arena of ethical self-realization for the citizen.

In Arendt's description, the political self is unreservedly a theatrical self, consumed with the passion for what she calls "greatness" and what Machiavelli described as glory. For her, greatness in human affairs flows from the desire to not only do well but to be the best among men. To achieve greatness, however, is not a matter of motive and aim which are, like "psychological qualities," universally the same for all men and therefore "never unique."[102] Motives and aims, irrespective of the authenticity or the moral purity of the persons concerned, cannot but appear to be similar in essence. Greatness in politics is the result, if at all, of the actual character and performance of action. In this sense, politics, in contrast to its aims and motives, is *sui generis*, in that action almost always produces unanticipated results. Following Pericles, Arendt insists that the "innermost meaning" of actions "is independent of victory or defeat, and must remain untouched by any eventual outcome, by (its) consequences for better or worse." To modern ears this is shocking counsel indeed. Human affairs conducted entirely in this way would make civilized life impossible. Arendt is clearly aware of this "moral" problem and she distinguishes between normal "human behaviour" which must be judged in terms of motives and consequences *and* action which is not bound by the moral limitations inherent in behaviour.[103] Normal behaviour includes all that men do when they serve necessity and utility, participate in family life and friendship, and are involved in quasi-political activities like legislation of laws and the administration of legal justice. Here moral standards are essential.

But in the political realm proper, composed exclusively of citizens unburdened by the more mundane considerations of life, human activity is to be judged by the excellence of the words and the deeds, not the consequences. The crucial distinction in this analysis is that between the public and the private realms. Since the public realm, in this ancient view, is the preserve of the public self, Arendt takes it for granted that ordinary moral standards are unnecessary. The ideal political self, that is to say, is uninterested in the kind of crassly necessitous and utilitarian competition characteristic of private, pre-political men. For us, accustomed as we are to the undifferentiated identity of politics and economics, it is essential to understand this difference.

For Arendt, then, politics is not for the sake of morality, nor are political and moral "ends" identical. Her view of politics, however, is not morally neutral or at least not divorced entirely from moral concerns, even though she drives hard the view of politics as an independent sphere of activity. According to Arendt, the moral standard appropriate in the realm of politics is forgiving.[104] The faculty of forgiving is a moral faculty in an oblique sense: it comes into play after the event. More importantly, it does not outlaw any action as immoral *a priori*. In terms of both the classical and modern view of morality, forgiving is evidently a marginal moral standard. Arendt asserts that the moral relevance of forgiving in political matters derives from the nature of the forgiving faculty itself. Forgiving is a moral code based on plurality, on "the presence of others." Forgiving is not something which one can do privately: "no one can forgive himself."[105] The one who forgives and the one who is forgiven are dependent on each other. Forgiving is a capacity which is rooted and arises in the realm of the "many:" it is irrelevant and impotent in the absence of others and it is not imposed on this realm from outside, as is the case with Platonic moral standards. Forgiving is in this sense an inherently political capacity for Arendt.

Forgiving is the proper remedy for action and its boundless and unpredictable effects, because without it men would be unable to act or not be able to act more than once:

> Without being forgiven, released from the consequences of what we have done, our capacity to act would, as it were, be confined to a single deed from which we could never recover; we would remain the victims of its consequences forever.[106]

To speak of being "victimized" by the consequences of one's own actions does indeed seem odd; but it is not odd at all, according to Arendt, since the consequences which flow from actions are invariably different, even opposed, to the original intentions. If the consequences of action require moral approval *a priori*, then there can be no freedom and no politics, since no action can be moral in the absolute sense or in the sense that it will not injure anyone. A degree of injurious and even criminal intent can be attributed, in principle, to almost all actions after the fact. The only guarantee of moral probity in the realm of human affairs is inaction or passivity.

Thus it is not strictly a question of morality versus immorality, but a matter of understanding the nature of political action as freedom. For Arendt as for Machiavelli, to distinguish the claims of politics from those of absolute morality is not to advocate evil: it is to recognize that public action is for the sake of excellence and glory. There is in fact more to it than that: this account of morality presupposes that evaluative standards and moral judgements are always part of particular social orders. What is right and wrong is intelligible in the context of the specific purposes of specific regimes. In this pre-modern understanding of morality lies the origin and justification of the moral characteristics of Arendt's political theory.

Having failed to argue this, she confounds the matter by invoking Kant. The most learned of modern moral theorists, Kant is justly famous for liberating the moral actor from subservience to wider social and political purposes. For Kant the actor is his own agent, not beholden to external authority, and as such he is the precise opposite of Arendt's public self. The fact that Kant as she says "had the courage to acquit man from the consequences of his deed"[107] is quite beside the point because he insisted that the actor's motives should be pure and that his fellow men should always be treated as ends, never as means.[108] Jealous of public honour and prestige, Arendt's actor fulfils neither of these requirements.

In the public realm, however, it is only action which is available and should be judged, not motives. This is right and proper, Arendt contends, because it is in the nature of motives to remain hidden "in the darkness of each man's lonely heart."[109]

PUBLIC SPACE AND HUMAN STATUS

In the *shared* human condition, there are just two possible and opposed ways of life: one is for the sake of "bodily" life itself; the other is for the sake of "worldly" life. The first is immanent and private; the second is transcendent and public. Arendt's key distinction between the private and the public perfectly describes the opposition between life and the world. This way of looking at the human condition is itself rooted in an intuitive pre-judgement in favour of the public world.

Underlying the two ways of life are radically different sensibilities: the truly human and the nearly beastly. The truly human is for Arendt the same as the public sensibility of the citizen-actor, whereas the nearly beastly she identifies with the private sensibility of the labourer. That there is a link between the kind of sensibility one has and what one does in life is not surprising. Labourers and the poor tend to value "privacy" in Arendt's sense just as the leisured citizens are likely to prize public things.[110] But there is in Arendt a contrary and more cogent view silently running through her theory; that sensibility is autonomous and independent of socio-economic circumstances. Now it can be argued that this contradicts an essential part of her theory: that the sensibility of the poor and the labouring classes is rooted in their condition of dire physical need; that their spirit is slavish and crudely necessitous;[111] that they do not and cannot know any better. Indeed Arendt ascribes the political failure of the French Revolution to the victory of the private sensibility of needs and wants of the liberated poor.[112]

This inconsistency would be fatal if her political theory were a species of philosophical materialism and if she had also proposed a material foundation for the public sensibility. This is in fact not the case. The causal link between sensibility and material circumstances is apparent only in the least advantaged of the labouring masses. One does not have to be a Marxist to see, as Arendt does, that the severely hungry and deprived will be preoccupied with "privacy" in her sense: food, clothing, and shelter. But as Arendt herself recognized this is not always true even in the case of the labouring poor,[113] and her own conviction that freedom is inherent in every man in virtue of his birth crucially supports the thesis that sensibility is autonomous. Further and indisputable, evidence for this thesis is supplied by another fundamental facet of her political theory: that the public realm can become unpolitical in substance, when informed by some version of the private sensibility preoccupied with individual or social interests. As Arendt sees it, this is precisely the fate of the public realm in modern liberal regimes.[114] Unless it is understood that the public and private sensibilities are largely autonomous, there can be no public realm since it serves no immediate pressing interest; conversely there can be a public realm without much trace of politics. There is no necessary reason why the public realm should be public in both form and content: it is a matter of inclination and disposition that it should be so. That is what the truly human sensibility will freely choose because to be political means "to attain the highest possibility of human existence."[115]

To be a public self, then, is to love the world, to believe that it is the world in which real "human" life is lived. When the world is suffused with freedom and action in her sense, it possesses the attribute of *worldliness*. As Arendt describes it, worldliness is a literary quality, the outcome of human relationships in which the world serves as the centre of meaningful speech; it is the result of actions which transcend private interest and private benefit. Worldliness entails active concern for what should and should not be allowed into the world.

Arendt's concern for the world is not a commitment to a "definite world view." With Lessing, she espouses what she calls the "viewpoint of the world."[116] The distinction is a fundamental one. Any world view is concerned with the realization of a certain kind of world, conceived in ideological or utilitarian terms. The modern world, in either its capitalist or communist version, is precisely a world built on a specific world view. To Arendt, this world is unworldly and monstrous because its impelling idea is rooted in the realm of need and mastery: the modern world is devoted to the satisfaction of necessity and utility, insensitive to the much less concrete and tangible claims of worldliness.

The attitude and mentality commensurate with the "viewpoint of the world," on the contrary, is one of independent judgement, consonant with the "needs" of the world.[117] This viewpoint "thinks," as it were, explicitly in terms of the "needs of the public realm."[118] From this public standpoint speech, action and freedom are primary; from the viewpoint of Nature, on the other hand, life, labour and necessity are primary.[119] From the latter viewpoint man has no history, survival is the ultimate aim, and human existence is nothing more than the cyclical recurrence of the species.

Arendt contends that the natural self is a necessitous, private and "worldless" creature.[120] He has little interest in tangible property, and none whatsoever in that elusive property: worldliness. Politically the natural self is a threat to the world and its worldliness because of his indifference to the space between men. His antipathy to the spatial dimension of life inheres in his inability to stand apart from Nature and from man *qua* man. The natural self automatically treats all men as fellow predators in the battle with necessity: he has no use for the space of appearance. Arendt asserts that this natural relationship literally eliminates the physical and human space between men.

Necessity is not the only root of *worldlessness*. Hostility to the world is historically characteristic of all groups existing on the periphery of society: that is, "enslaved groups and persecuted peoples." For example, the European Jews, according to Arendt, living on the margins of Western society, had always shared a close "humanity in the form of fraternity" which served to undermine real interest in the world.[121] Naturally the Jews were more concerned with their communal survival than with the condition of the world. For Arendt, the fact of the matter—quite apart from the reasons which shaped this attitude—is that the Jews existed as a worldless, pariah group. The same thing can be said essentially of all minority groups existing on the edge of society. From the viewpoint of politics, the pariah is a dangerous person: his sole interest is his own well-being and that of his ethnic community. The world as the space of relationships neither attracts his attention nor merits his concern. Arendt is convinced that such "worldlessness" is not only anti-political, but "always a form of barbarism."[122] Anti-worldliness is barbaric in the specific sense that it refuses to recognize the reality of anything but its immediate, private and pressing interests. On this level at least, Homer's cyclops, Conrad's "black savages," and segments of nineteenth century European Jewry stand condemned together as worldless and "inhuman" people.

In the modern world, Arendt asserts, worldlessness has become a universal fact of human life: the problem with modern man is not self-alienation but world-alienation.[123] Indeed, it is not the world which lies at the core of modern concerns but the private self and the needs and wants of personal life. That "life is the highest good" is the self-evident and unrelenting premise of almost all social thought in the modern age.[124] Marx stands out as the most articulate and learned proponent of this view. In modern philosophy as well, the primacy of the private self is paramount: since Descartes, philosophy has been exclusively concerned with "the self, as distinguished from the soul or person or man in general."[125] This preoccupation with the self signals an explicit retreat from the world and other men, into the sphere of experience relevant to isolated, separated men. Arendt knows that withdrawal from the world is not a new phenomenon. Our tradition of philosophy originated in precisely such despair with the existing world. But the ancient philosopher turned away from the apparent world to "another world of eternal truth," from which he returned to re-order the actual world.[126] Plato remains the supreme example of the philosopher who discovered the transcendent truth, yet he was sufficiently concerned about the world to attempt to change it.

In contrast, modern philosophers and soon after, modern men, turned away both from the actual world and the world of eternal truth, into themselves. The modern mind is defined by its passion for introspection, "the cognitive concern of consciousness with its own content . . . [where] man is confronted with nothing and nobody but himself."[127] At the heart of the introspective mentality is the seminal inability to be part of the common and public world. In fact this mentality, according to Arendt, is not bound by *common* sense or *common* experiences: it is a private, self-indulgent mentality unconcerned with the "relationship between man and the world."[128] Indeed the world and other people appear as entities which threaten the individual and disturb his peace of mind. Thus it is entirely in character for modern philosophy and modern man to show an inordinate interest in the "theory of cognition and psychology." For the latter are the intellectual pursuits of men severed from each other and from the world.[129]

This concern for the individual self is also patent in modern political theory. From Hobbes down to Mill, the primacy of the self and its well-being is the sacred canon of political argument. Perhaps it is true to say that in the liberal-democratic thought of Bentham and Mill, the relationship between man and the social world receives more attention than it does in the political theories of Hobbes and Locke. But here as well, the individual self and his security remains the dominant focus of interest. French existential thought, at least in its Sartrean version, also attests to the preeminent role of the individual self in modern thought. Indeed, this is the meaning of Sartre's much quoted statement, that for the individual self "Hell is other people."

In Arendt's eyes, the undisputed priority of the private, psychological self in modern thought is only the obverse of modernity's hostility to politics and the world. The modern age marks the fall of public man and the rise of the psychological self to the position of honour in the public mind. Ironically, Marx's charge, that self-alienation was the central moral and personal problem of the modern age, was levelled against a liberal society that had liberated the self not only from its traditional privacy but from politics as well.[130] Marx's unconcern with the "world" in her sense was far more intense than that shown by any of the liberal thinkers. Marx understood alienation as the enforced incapacity of man to appropriate and enjoy products of his own making. According to Arendt, Marx meant that "the things of the world, once they have been produced by men, are to an extent independent of, 'alien' to, human life."[131] In this interpretation Marx objected to the existence of an independent world as alienating.

Since Marx's concept of alienation is an integral part of his critique of the systematic injustice of the capitalist mode of production, Arendt's judgement may seem unfair to Marx.[132] From her public point of view, nevertheless, it is still true that Marxian thought is anti-worldly. Marx was unmistakably uninterested in the world as a durable and independent community of things and deeds. [133] For Marx, the secret motor of the human condition was the way in which men strove to satisfy their needs and wants. Human actions, products and ideas were not explicable in terms of other ideas unconnected with practical life.

In the radically distinct attitudes of Arendt and Marx to the world lie the essential difference between her *political* thought and his *social* thought. For Marx, man is naturally a social creature, and all human life is social life. To speak of individual man apart from society is to utter nonsense: "the individual *is* the *social being*." Individual life is an instance of species-life and "the particular individual is only a *determinate species-being*." [134] In the Marxian view, the world of Arendt or, for that matter, the "liberal" world, concretely reflects the separation of man from his species-life. Insofar as this world stresses the separation of man from man, and not their natural unity, human relationships resemble relationships between isolated entities. For Marx this world testifies to the gap that exists between the individual and society and between the private and the public self. Individualism and politics thrive on this fundamental and antithetical dichotomy between man and man, and man and the world. To eliminate alienation is to rescue man from this pernicious individuality, to deprive the world of its autonomy and to close the gap between the private individual and social man. For Marx, the challenge is to restore to the separate, political individual his original unity with other men, that is, his social being.

In contrast, the problem for Arendt is to re-open the gap between the individual and society, to separate the private and the public self, to re-discover the world as the space between men. For her man is "a 'social' before he is a 'political' animal." [135] Life in the social realm is pre-political, in that it is centred around activities essential to "sustain life." For the ancients, as well as for Arendt, Marx's social vision signals a retreat from public-political life of freedom into the life of the household and its urgent necessity. Marx abolishes the distinction between the public and the private, crucial to politics, and sanctions the collective pursuit of private needs and aims in public: "it is the life-process itself which in one form or another has been channelled into the public realm." [136] From Arendt's political standpoint, it is not difficult to see that, contrary to Marx, it is world-alienation and not self-alienation which "has been the hallmark of the modern age." [137]

In Marx, it is still the private self in his social guise who thrives in the public realm. While this self is a public creature in the sense that he secures his life-interest in the public realm, he is not a political or a worldly self. For Arendt, Marxian man, in spite of his emergence into the light of the public, is essentially a natural creature, tied to necessity. Her critique of the modern view of the self as a private, unworldly creature leads us to the heart of her novel conception of the relationship between public space and human status; between politics and the individual self. In the public realm "men can show who they really and inexchangeably" are.[138] In no other activity is this possible, because men are burdened with other considerations of life. But in this realm man has the chance to present himself as a "who," not just a "what" — "his qualities, gifts, talents and shortcomings."[139] The distinction between "what" and "who" somebody is, is a critical one.

Traditionally, definitions of man as a unique being have invariably posited certain qualities which mark him out. Human nature in its normative sense has been identified with the chosen qualities man possesses or ought to possess in his maturity. Hence human status has in the past been assigned on the basis of these qualities, moral or otherwise. For Arendt, isolation of such qualities tells us "what" man is or ought to be, but never "who" he is. Describing his qualities identifies a man's character but still "his specific uniqueness escapes us," because "the moment we want to say *who* somebody is, our vocabulary leads us astray into saying *what* he is."[140] In both the classical and the modern view moral man and natural man, respectively, are defined in terms of such qualities.

Arendt contends that who man is, or who a particular man is, transcends his combined heritage of qualities and talents: it is in action in the public realm that man shows "who" he is. His unique identity is the result of his overt performance, which may or may not reveal all of his personal qualities. Furthermore, his identity is not fully apparent until he dies. To say this is to say that who man is, is intimately related to the use he makes of his freedom to act. In this conception, *animal laborans*, whose mode of life is inherently unfree, and *homo faber*, who believes that a "man's products may be more . . . than himself,"[141] cannot reveal themselves as separate, unique persons, as individuals in the proper meaning of the term. For the ancients as for Arendt, action remains the highest capacity, because the political realm is strictly "*reserved for individuality*."[142] Authentic human identity is not predicated on productive activity or contemplative inactivity, but on forceful action in word and deed in the shared arena of politics, where men insert themselves as singular persons in the communal mind.

On this level as well, it becomes clear why Plato's moral man and Marx's natural man evoke Arendt's political ire. In different ways, both types of men are anti-worldly, suspicious of the free and assertive individual and hence hostile to politics for its own sake. The liberal man fares better in this frame of judgement, because he still sets much store by worldly property and freedom, even though the liberal view of freedom is not political.[143] In passing, Arendt even praises this freedom: "one of the most important negative liberties we have enjoyed since the end of the ancient world, namely, freedom from politics."[144]

In public action, then, man reveals who he is, in his words and deeds. Some measure of self-revelation is implicit in everything men do and its absence would indicate "complete silence and perfect passivity."[145] But for Arendt a man cannot be said to have revealed himself unless he explicitly ventures into the public realm. True action, however, presupposes a human being, and an actor disinclined to speak or conduct himself in speech has renounced both his human peculiarity and the claim to human status. Such an actor represents the antithesis of action, inasmuch as he refuses to avail himself of the only faculty denied to other species: namely speech. A deed without words is not action, but violence; deeds without words are humanly and politically barren. For it is the distinctive mark of politics that it thrives on speech and persuasion.

By identifying action with speech, Arendt intends to dissociate it radically from violence. Violence is speechless in the sense that violence begins where speech ends. Violence uses implements: it is "distinguished by its instrumental character." In contrast, action is performed in speech, directly as it were, without the aid of tools. Violence and action denote entirely different ways of organized living: the one is political, the other its opposite. Violence is a method of commanding and dictating obedience; action is a method of acting and eliciting agreement among equals.[146] Thus politics as action excludes violence, though politics is not possible unless some men are forced to assure the satisfaction of communal needs and wants. In the public realm itself, violence is illegitimate without qualification, though it is, apparently, deemed necessary by Arendt to the founding of the polity. From her viewpoint, this is the human price to be paid for humanizing men and the world in her sense.

Arendt's the public self, her true citizen, simultaneously acts in radically opposed ways. In the household, he resorts to violence and domination; in the public realm, he forsakes violence for speech. Violence, however, remains the underlying motif of political action in two senses. Arendt maintains that citizenship requires that the actor be continuously violent in the private sphere of his life. To abandon violence is to risk subjugation by others, loss of freedom, and hence the possibility of action and politics. In the public realm, the public self is obliged to be continuously assertive. Though he is an equal among equals, the public self is "highly individualistic:" he strives to be the first even in this gathering of equals. In this view, the political self is, if not violent, certainly forceful and aggressive "at the expense of all other factors."[147] Even his equals suffer injury and insult at the hands of the public self. In all his bloody magnificence, Achilles remains the "paradigmatic" instance of this type of political action.[148] In Homer's graphic description, Achilles emerges as a petulant, insensitive and unyielding personality, careless in injuring and offending, indeed besting, his compatriots as well as his enemies. Arendt sees Achilles as the finest example of the authentic public self in the literature of the West. Achilles is the man in the heroic mould, the agonal spirit, driven to excel, to be the first among men. Arendt stresses Achilles' love of the public realm and public excellence, his public sensibility, as his outstanding trait.

For Arendt, the self's individuality and identity depends on his active appearance in public. Sheer audibility and visibility are not enough. To establish individuality, he must do something in the common world: he must explicitly disclose himself, in action, to others.[149]

To appear in the world is to do so in the requisite space of appearance — the public-political arena. This view of human individuality is quite opposed to the idea of individuality ennucleated in modern psychology: it has nothing to do with contemporary notions of self-expression or the self-willed identity, in its existential or other versions. Individuality is always "actualized" and affirmed in public intercourse. For Arendt, the individual can appear as singularly "one" only in public. Personality or personal uniqueness, what she also describes as "the living essence of the person," really "appears and is visible only to others:"[150] it is not a matter of self-decision or self-recommendation. Self-interpretation is always illusory because it lacks a meaningful relationship with the world and other people. The real self — or at least as far as it is possible to know this self — is the public or political self. Unless the self presents himself in a relationship "man *qua* man" in the public realm, neither is his existence affirmed, nor is his personality actualized.[151] In this purely human relationship, the necessitous and utilitarian concerns of life are out of order. But both the human relationship and the human personality are inconceivable if the individual remains in his self-validating privacy: private man is "natural" man, neither human nor real. Arendt sees little difference between privacy and fantasy and privacy and the loss of reality: "private man does not appear and it is as though he did not exist."[152]

Arendt's insistence on the need for public revelation is a necessary outcome of her "metaphysical" view of death. Politics in the sense of appearance attests to the fact that men are alive and free and worldly creatures. In this basic and perhaps obvious sense, politics is the opposite of death, in that politics facilitates and encourages meaningful communal life. In her own words: "death is perhaps the most anti-political experience there is. . . . For the living, death is primarily dis-appearance."[153] For Arendt, death is the same as non-Being, and Being is more or less identical with revealing oneself publicly. Politics is the metaphysical vindication of human being, in that politics is the proximate ground of Being:

in politics, more than anywhere else, we have no possibility of distinguishing between being and appearance. In the realm of human affairs, being and appearance are indeed one and the same.[154]

In this context, Arendt's attitude towards slavery is illuminating. That slavery is unjust and inhumane is true but it is the necessary condition of politics and culture. For her the crucial point about slavery is not its challenge to morality, but the fact that slave-status denies men the chance to "appear" at all in the world. Slavery hides some men permanently from the public arena. Essentially the same is true of all men, slaves or the poor, who have no choice but to toil ceaselessly for their needs and wants and those of others. Indeed, Arendt holds that "darkness rather than want is the curse of poverty" and slavery.[155] Clearly, this is significant only from the viewpoint of politics. Slaves and poor men burdened with the cares of life cannot appear in the light of the public space and establish their unique identities.

Slavery and poverty are forms of death: neither condition allows one to stake one's claim to humanity, to appear as a singular individual. Stated differently, politics interests men who object to the futility and mortality of individual life. Slaves and poor men are human types who are not bothered by the darkness of their condition—or at least not bothered enough—to seek to transcend their penurious and beastly state of life. In positive terms, politics as action and appearance attracts free men authentically concerned with earthly immortality. This is another way of saying that men contemptuous of mere life are the most worldly and the most political of men. Arendt recognizes this to be the unique and striking characteristic of ancient politics:

For the *polis* was for the Greeks, as the *res publica* was for the Romans, first of all their guarantee against the futility of individual life, the space protected against this futility and reserved for the relative permanence, if not immortality, of mortals.[156]

When she speaks of politics, it is this space reserved for immortal speech and deeds which she fervently seeks to restore. To be political is also to believe that there are things worth conversing about, that conversation itself is a worthwhile activity, and that relationships which lie outside the pale of civic conversation are not fully human.

For Arendt, the identity of humanity and politics inheres in her view that politics brings into play free men devoted to free speech in the presence of other free men, entirely for the sake of "the truly human dialogue . . . permeated by pleasure in the other person and what he says."[157] This does not mean that the individual political actor is not moved by jealousy, fear or even hatred. Indeed, the public self, in Arendt's description, is intensely proud and driven to outshine his peers at every opportunity. But it does mean that, no matter how aggressive or offensive the political actor becomes, he can be certain that the character of his performance will be noticed and appreciated. For this plurality of peers shares a common commitment to public excellence in speech and deed: "the specifically human way of answering and talking back and measuring up to whatever happened or was done . . . finding the right words at the right moment."[158] What is crucial to notice here is that, while action is the attribute of a particular actor, speech and deeds become excellent in the company of men who relish his performance and participate in the drama unleashed by him. Human excellence is always a public affair, even though it is a personal achievement. The glorious actor acquires excellence in the minds and the memory of his fellow participants. Only in this sense can he be said to have done well, to have appeared, to have established his "unchangeable identity."[159]

In her emphasis on the public nature of excellence lies another critical facet of her view of politics. The public sphere alone is the source of reality for men, in that it is the judgement of the common realm which enables human beings to be certain that what they do is not illusory and unreal. Arendt insists that reality, or what must pass for reality in the human condition, is to be had in the public and shared space of politics: "To be deprived of it means to be deprived of reality, which, humanly and politically speaking, is the same as appearance."[160] Reality is not the same as truth: it is the democratic judgement of the many or the citizens as to the validity and appropriateness of whatever appears in the public realm. Politics in this sense is the human measure of reality: anything else, because it "lacks this appearance" in this public space "is intimately and exclusively our own but without reality," that is without significance to others.[161]

For Arendt, it is the privative nature of his biological and social life and his introspective turn of mind which trap the modern self in the circular realm of illusion and deception, without consequence to the world and other people. The product of this state of affairs is the "modern individual and his endless conflicts," unable "either to be at home in society or to live altogether outside it."[162] In contrast, it is in action, in the practice of politics in her sense, that man achieves the highest and most sought-after prizes in human existence: action simultaneously yields reality, confirms personality, promises excellence, and makes human life meaningful. The public dimension of human life redeems life's natural futility and endows the historical doings of men with meaning.

For this it is necessary that men have faith in and trust other men in their relationships and encounters in the world:

> without a space of appearance and without trusting in action and speech as a mode of being together, neither the reality of one's self, of one's identity, nor the reality of the surrounding world can be established beyond doubt.[163]

Whether this worldly reality can ever be "established beyond doubt" is a moot question. Still, what is certain is that without others "who see what we see and hear what we hear,"[164] we are unable to distinguish between the real and the unreal, the excellent and the mediocre, and the permanent and the fleeting, in our lives. In short, outside the shared realm of politics the human hold on reality, individual identity, and excellence becomes even more tenuous and uncertain.

Arendt knows that her claims on behalf of politics are unusual. In all other respects, the domain of politics does indeed seem like "a battlefield of partial, conflicting interests, where nothing counted but pleasure and profit."[165] While this is true of all politics part of the time, politics is not politics unless it allows men to act and speak, to be free and bold in the public realm. In a later work, Arendt writes that politics and political freedom "generally speaking, means the right to be a participator in government."[166] But for her this choice is unarguably the second-best and in no sense does this concession dilute her passion for politics in the ancient Greek sense.[167]

Arendt's nuanced and circumscribed vision of politics stands starkly opposed to the modern understanding of politics. In her view, the public self can neither be happy, nor should he seek after happiness, the end so central to the modern conception. If happiness may be defined as general contentment which arises from a life lived with some measure of certainty about the future, the public-political man will never feel this happiness. Such happiness is the ideal of *animal laborans* or natural man, a happiness intimately associated with the natural "rhythms" of social or bodily life; "the man of action" has never demanded "to be 'happy' or thought that mortal men could be happy"[168] in this sense.

Austere and disciplined, Arendt's public self not only does not crave happiness, his manner of life is fraught with personal suffering. As an actor, he does many things which necessarily cause him to suffer from the consequences of his action: for "to do and suffer are like opposite sides of the same coin."[169] This image of man and action is a familiar one in ancient Greek tragedy: the public self is a tragic as well as a theatrical self. Though Arendt does not say so, he is a tragic self in two specific senses. He has cultivated the ability to act and suffer with grace and honour. He accepts suffering with the dignity of a man who knows the prickly texture of the human condition and the inevitability with which man is subjected to deserved and undeserved insult and injury.

Secondly, the tragic aspect of the political self is inherent in the fact that until he acts, he cannot know what he will reveal to the world and, more importantly, to himself about himself. Before he acts, the actor is unknown to the world and to himself; self-knowledge is knowledge acquired in the performance of action. The Socratic maxim "know thyself" is here redefined to mean, know thyself in action in relation to other men and the world. For to know oneself in privacy and isolation is not to know the real but the imaginary self. Self-knowledge is thus political knowledge in the peculiar sense that the self comes to know himself in action in the public realm, in the presence of fellow men, for better or worse.

Self-knowledge in the political sense is fundamentally different from the modern psychoanalytic route to knowledge. Psychoanalysis is a mode of epistemological inquiry which attempts to unveil the ostensibly hidden sources of truth about man in terms of precisely those things which man is unwilling to reveal about himself. Arendt impatiently dismisses the modern battery of psychoanalysis and depth-psychology as being no more than a species of "curiosity-seeking."[170] For her, this kind of knowledge is pseudo-knowledge, based on the false expectation that what lurks in the human heart can be known if one tries hard enough. The heart is that dark and privileged region harbouring the innermost subjective thoughts and feelings of each man; according to Arendt, these are legitimately private and should be left alone.

Literary critic Harold Rosenberg's reflections on action succinctly capture the opposed impulses animating the public self of Arendt and the psychological sensibility of the modern self: "what makes psychoanalysis the opposite of tragedy . . . is that the sufferer hands over to another — the analyst — the process of disclosing who he is, instead of struggling toward self-knowledge through action."[171] For Rosenberg as for Arendt, though she does not mention him, the real self is the public and, in the literary sense, tragic self who has the courage to risk knowledge about himself in worldly action and suffer the consequences on his own. As Aristotle remarked, what counts in tragedy is not character but action; to be more precise, character is inferred from action. Tragedy is concerned with men of action as much better than they really are, that is nobler and more distinguished.[172] This is precisely the patrician view of man which accurately describes Arendt's ideal public actor and citizen.

To depict Arendt's theory as a rival account of politics and the public realm falls far short of the mark: it should be apparent that her project entails a radically different account of the nature and substance of politics. There is no reason to think that she did not believe in all that she says is at stake in the public realm. Still, the literary-dramatic character of her public realm and her citizen-actors raises the question whether she has not fallen prey to aesthetics and consequently confused politics with aesthetics. For it is clear that the "great words and deeds" in her public realm bear an uncanny resemblance to "action" on the theatrical stage. The crucial difference of course is that in the theatre we witness pure enactment, in the public realm we encounter pure action: the one cannot be transposed wholesale into the other without denaturing both the theatre and politics. There is also the moral risk involved in mistaking the dramatic word for the deed and in substituting the word for the deed. Plato and Rousseau were intent on banishing play-actors from their *Republics* partially for this reason. Neither of them could see anything *morally* valuable in the literary arts of drama and poetry as integral constituents of the public realm.

To this objection Arendt's reply would be that both Plato and Rousseau had confounded politics with morality. That she is essentially right is not reason enough to accept her account of politics in its entirety. This needs to be stressed because her passion for the literary-dramatic in public life does not commit her to a view of citizen-actors as accomplished aesthetes engaged in an aesthetic ritual for its own sake. The resemblance not-withstanding, public citizenship entails much more than aesthetic satisfaction. Arendt prizes it because it is the source of the human sense of reality and personal identity; it attests to the fact of human freedom and it saves man from the insipid and unceasing futility of mere life. This is the substantial core of her public realm, stripped of its excess theatrical dressing.

Undoubtedly there is considerable truth in this understanding of the public realm. The doubt that remains concerns the principles of public action: whether the principles of honour, glory, distinction and hatred[173] are not so self-interested as to be subvert rather than sustain and care for the public realm? The obvious answer is that the end result is contingent on the strength of the public sensibility of the political actor: this after all is the realm of freedom, there can be no guarantees here. But can there not be some version of positive morality consistent with public action and with the distinction between politics and morality traditionally understood? There is a relevant argument to be found on this question in Arendt's theory, although she does not make it herself.

NOTES

1 *HC*: 57, 174.
2 Ibid.: 10-11.
3 Ibid.: 157-158.
4 Ibid.: 10.
5 *BPF*: 153.
6 Ibid.: 148.
7 Ibid.: 146.
8 Ibid.: 148.
9 Ibid.: 149.
10 Ibid.: 148.
11 Ibid.: 147.
12 Ibid.: 146.
13 Maurice Cranston has suggested that Arendt is a metaphysical existentialist; a philosophical position, he goes on to add, "which can go together with a variety of beliefs in politics and morals." This is certainly true of Heidegger but quite untrue in Arendt's case, as I have tried to show in the course of this study. Cranston also confuses Arendt's notion of freedom with the existentialist notion of inner freedom; cf. his remarks in *Encounter* (March 1976): 54-56.
14 See, for example, Heidegger, *What is Called Thinking?* (New York, 1972) and Sartre, *Being and Nothingness* (New York, 1966). For Albert Camus' differing view of freedom, see *The Rebel* (New York, 1956).
15 See his *Early Writings*, ed. T. B. Bottomore (New York, 1964), the essays on the Jewish Question.
16 *BPF*: 151.
17 Ibid.: 152.
18 Ibid.: 157-158.
19 Ibid.: 167.
20 *HC*: 215.
21 Ibid.: 222.
22 *BPF*: 161-162.
23 *HC*: 157-158.
24 *VLE*: 82.
25 *HC*: 27.
26 Ibid.: 159, 162, *passim*.
27 *REV*: 9.
28 *HC*: 177.
29 Ibid.: 162, 48.
30 Ibid.: 163.
31 For a discussion of this critical facet of totalitarian rule, see Ch. 5 of this study.
32 See Arendt's review of concentration camp literature in *Commentary* (Sept. 1946): 291-295.
33 *HC*: 162.
34 Ibid.: 24; Hegel's very similar view is to be found in *The Phenomenology of Mind* (New York, 1967): 342-343, 349. Arendt does not refer to Hegel's argument in this context.
35 *HC*: 156.
36 Ibid.: 210.

37 Ibid.: 44.
38 Ibid.: 31.
39 Ibid.: 292-294.
40 *BPF*: 165.
41 Ibid.: 171.
42 *HC*: 169.
43 Ibid.: 206-207.
44 Ibid.: 171.
45 Ibid.: 170.
46 Ibid.: 171.
47 Ibid.: 212-213.
48 Ibid.: 163, contrary to the mistaken view of Margaret Canovan and Bhikhu Parekh.
    Both think that Arendt laments modern man's inability to control and shape his life:
    see *The Political Thought of Hannah Arendt* (London, 1974): 77; and "Hannah Arendt's
    Critique of Marx" in *Hannah Arendt: Recovery of the Public World*, ed. M. A. Hill (New
    York, 1979): 69, 76, respectively.
49 *HC*: 164.
50 Ibid.: 220.
51 Ibid.: 210.
52 *BPF*: 164.
53 *HC*: 210.
54 This view is implicit in Arendt's scattered remarks on these thinkers, in her work; see in
    particular *HC*: 90, 112, 113, 145, 165, 174, 175, 197-206, 231, *passim* and *REV*:
    56-58, 72, 73-75, *passim*.
55 *HC*: 197.
56 Ibid.: 199.
57 Ibid.: 79, 330-331.
58 *BPF*: 79.
59 *HC*: 206.
60 Ibid.: 205.
61 Ibid.: 211.
62 *BPF*: 165; cf. *REV*: 152.
63 *HC*: 102; this is Veblen's phrase.
64 *Symposium*, 208d.
65 *HC*: 33.
66 Ibid.: 84-85.
67 Ibid.: 177-178.
68 Ibid.: 59.
69 *BPF*: 156.
70 Ibid.: 152.
71 *HC*: 157.
72 *BPF*: 152.
73 *HC* 159-160.
74 *OR*: 31, 67, *passim*.
75 *BPF*: 152.
76 *HC*: 172.
77 See their articles in the collection edited by DeLamar Jensen, *Machiavelli* (Boston,
    1966).

78 Ibid.: xv.
79 *Thoughts on Machiavelli* (Seattle, 1958): 10.
80 Ibid.: 12.
81 *BPF*: 137.
82 Ibid.: 137.
83 *REV*: 97.
84 *BPF*: 137.
85 *HC*: 202.
86 *BPF*: 137.
87 Ibid.: 138.
88 Ibid.: 137.
89 *CR*: 62.
90 *REV*: 29.
91 Ibid.: 290.
92 Ibid.
93 *HC*: 35.
94 *BPF*: 137.
95 Ibid.: 153.
96 Ibid.: 137.
97 See Alasdair MacIntyre, *A Short History of Ethics* (New York, 1966), Ch. 2.
98 *BPF*: 153.
99 *HC*: 185.
100 Ibid.: 167.
101 Rousseau's criticisms of the theatre and the theatrical self constitute the bulk of his well-known essay on the theatre: *Politics and the Arts*, ed. A. Bloom (New York, 1960).
102 *HC*: 185.
103 Ibid.: 184.
104 Ibid.: 212.
105 Ibid.: 213-214.
106 Ibid.: 213.
107 Ibid.: 361.
108 Kant, *Foundations of the Metaphysics of Morals* (Indianapolis, 1959).
109 *HC*: 213.
110 Ibid.: 114, 115, *passim*; *REV*: 41, 54, *passim*.
111 See M. Canovan, "The Contradictions of Hannah Arendt's Political Thought," *Political Theory* 6, 1 (Feb. 1978): 11; in his response to Canovan, Martin Levin rightly says that Arendt attacks the labouring mentality, not the labouring poor: cf. his "On *Animal Laborans* and *Homo Politicus* in Hannah Arendt," *Political Theory* 7, 4 (Nov. 1979): 524.
112 *REV*, esp. Ch. II; *HC*: 58, 74.
113 *HC*: 195.
114 Ibid., Ch. VI, sections 44, 45.
115 Ibid.: 58.
116 *MDT*: 8.
117 Ibid.
118 Arendt, in a discussion during the Conference on her thought at York University, November 1972 (from my notes).
119 *HC*: 80-87.
120 Ibid.: 233.

121 *MDT*: 13.
122 Ibid.
123 *HC*: 231.
124 Ibid.: 291.
125 Ibid.: 230.
126 Ibid.: 267.
127 Ibid.: 254.
128 Ibid.: 255.
129 Ibid.: 267.
130 Ibid.: 231.
131 Ibid.: 328.
132 Ibid., Ch. III.
133 This crucial point has been missed by commentators who have addressed Arendt's critique of Marx; for instance, Bhikhu Parekh and Robert Major in their essays in *Hannah Arendt*, ed. M. A. Hill: 67-100 and 131-156, respectively.
134 *Early Writings*, ed. T. B. Bottomore: 158-159.
135 *HC*: 30.
136 Ibid.: 42-43.
137 Ibid.: 231.
138 Ibid.: 38.
139 Ibid.: 159.
140 Ibid.: 161.
141 Ibid.: 186.
142 Ibid.: 38 (emphasis added).
143 *CR*: 221, and *REV*: 284.
144 *REV*: 284.
145 *HC*: 159.
146 *VLE*: 46-47.
147 *HC*: 173.
148 Ibid.: 173.
149 Ibid.: 166.
150 Ibid.: 161, 172.
151 Ibid.: 186; George Kateb makes the same point in his perceptive study, *Hannah Arendt: Conscience, Politics, Evil* (Oxford, 1984), Ch. 1: 8.
152 *HC*: 54.
153 *VLE*: 67; *HC*: 315.
154 *REV*: 93-94.
155 Ibid.: 64.
156 *HC*: 51.
157 *MDT*: 15.
158 *HC*: 26-27.
159 Ibid.: 172.
160 Ibid.: 178.
161 Ibid.: 176-179.
162 Ibid.: 36.
163 Ibid.: 187.
164 Ibid.: 46.
165 *BPF*: 263.

166 *REV*: 221.
167 This is little evidence to support Peter Fuss' claim that Arendt repudiated her "agonal" conception in favor of an accommodational view of politics in her later writings: see "Hannah Arendt's Conception of Political Community" in *Hannah Arendt*, ed. M. A. Hill: 172.
168 *HC*: 115.
169 Ibid.: 169.
170 *RAHEL*: xviii.
171 *Act and the Actor* (New York, 1970): 63.
172 Aristotle, *Poetics*, Chs. 13 and 15, in *Classical Literary Criticism* (Harmondsworth, 1978).
173 *BPF*: 152.

CHAPTER FIVE

Morality and politics

FOR ARENDT THE CLAIMS of morality and moral life on politics and human affairs are much less self-evident and much more ambivalent than they were for Plato. In his political writings Plato leaves no doubt that life in the polity is for the purpose of making men moral. The political association is in essence an educative set of institutions designed to improve the moral and human stature of men. Plato's citizens are first and foremost good and virtuous both in their activities and in their thoughts. The end for classical men is refinement in virtue, that is knowledge, of the Good. For Plato the good citizen is identical with the good man: political man is moral man.

In Aristotle's less rigorous and much more subtle understanding of the *polis* as a mixture of "unlike elements," the excellence of the citizen does not depend solely on his moral goodness. A man can be a good citizen without necessarily being a good man. Good citizenship does not require the "single absolute excellence" characteristic of the truly good man.[1] For Aristotle the good man and good citizen are identical only in the good, that is the ideal, state.

Aristotle's distinction is particularly significant in that he allows that citizenship is not primarily a moral vocation, although the moral nature of the ultimate goal he neither doubts nor denies. Aristotle corrects Plato's account not at the expense of morality but in favour of a realistic appraisal of the worldly nature of political life. Arendt's understanding of politics is rooted in the Aristotelian distinction between the good man and the good citizen, between morality and politics.[2] But it is by no means identical with it, either in terms of Aristotle's fundamental moral intent or in terms of the duties of citizenship. Unlike Aristotle, Arendt does not see citizenship simply as participation in the administrative, legislative and legal affairs of the *polis*. Indeed, as we have seen, her concern is more with action, freedom and the display of individual excellence in the public-political arena.

Notes to Chapter Five appear on page 139.

In Aristotelian terms, Arendt's citizens can be described as citizens only in a marginal sense. They lack the moral fervour and the passion for virtue essential to classical candidates for citizenship. This is not an accidental difference. Arendt's citizens are quintessentially actors, public men in the heroic mould, the spiritual progeny of Achilles. They are not good men, nor are they meant to be. They are men possessed of the agonal spirit, impatient with ordinary standards of goodness and morality in pursuit of glory.

Arendt's citizens may not be moral men in the classical sense but they are not immoral. Her polity and her public men belong to a moral community in two specific senses. First, the public life of citizenship constitutes a moral choice freely made by men who could easily have chosen otherwise: their purpose being to establish and sustain the public realm. That this genre of assertive citizenship issues in conduct often damaging and detrimental to others is not sufficient ground to label it as immoral. If the morality of public conduct is at issue, then it can plausibly be argued that public men of this sort injure others far less than citizens engaged in the venal life of trade and profit.

Secondly, the political association Arendt has in mind is a moral community, in that it is based on trust, friendship and mutual concern.[3] The fate of other citizens and the character of public life are dear to public men. Thus in a crucial sense the polity is a moral association drawing its energy from the bonds of respect inhering in friendship and trust for one another, which derive from an original trust in men. Without this measure of trust and generous friendship the political realm cannot exist. The "sharing of words and deeds" between citizens who enjoy an equivalence of equality and therefore respect among themselves, is the essence of common public life.[4] In this sense the life of citizenship is certainly a moral life.

It is clear that Arendt assumes this to be true of her public realm, an assumption without which her conception of the public realm as the locus of human excellence is unintelligible. But the moral calibre of this association is evidently weak and tepid. For she is committed neither to the moral "ought" (categorical imperative) of Kant, nor to the classical conception of virtue and the good life as the moral life. From her "public" and "external" point of view, a vigorous attachment to Kantian and classical morality is not only incompatible with, but destructive of, freedom and action and therefore of the public realm and the public self. In either version, this is the internal morality of "man in the singular:"[5] it is the ideal of man preoccupied with saving his soul. Such a man can never be concerned with politics as intrinsically worthy in itself.

There seems to be something drastically wrong with this account of politics. Can Arendt be seriously saying that conventional morality has no

place in her public realm? This surely must be a misreading of her position!
There is no mistake: she is intent on severing the established link between
conventional morality and politics because she believes such morality to be
fatally dangerous to human beings, especially in times of crises. Three
instances in her writings seem to me essential to understanding her complex
and novel view of morality in the public realm: her reflections on *Billy
Budd*, on aspects of the French Revolution and on the case of Eichmann. In
each case her standard of judgement is that of the public realm.

BILLY BUDD

Arendt reads Melville's *Billy Budd* as a profound political tale whose central
theme is the nature of the public realm and the kind of disposition it
requires of those who would be citizens. Billy Budd is a unique figure in the
context of Melville's story. Billy is not conversant with public affairs and
lacks understanding of the reasons he should learn the ropes of political
conduct. Arendt legitimately sees him as a contemporary Jesus returned "to
the world of men,"[6] the tangible incarnation not merely of goodness but of
absolute goodness in a mundane setting. In her eyes, Billy is absolutely
good because he is absolutely innocent; his is the innocence of nature, not of
calculation. Neither his background—he was a foundling—nor his
intentions—he could not hide his feelings—reveal a past of experience, an
historical identity. The world with its ready complement of conflicts and
lies seems to have missed him and he has remained as innocent as he was at
birth.

Though Billy's mates are bewildered and bemused by his good nature,
they neither despise nor cross him. Arendt intimates that in the ordinary
course of events Billy would have continued to survive in his innocent
privacy without encountering serious difficulties. Claggart's forceful intrusion, however, darkens and eventually shatters this idyllic state of affairs.
Naturally and relentlessly evil, Claggart is intensely irked by goodness of
any kind, in his mind an attribute intrinsically out of order in the com-
promising world of men. To Claggart absolute goodness poses a serious
challenge to his conservatively anxious assessment of man as basically evil.
Billy's goodness forcefully represents the denial of its contrary. In Arendt's
reading, Claggart as the bearer of evil is compelled to destroy Billy: he fears
the reputed power of goodness. Inevitably Claggart accuses Billy of serious
insubordination. Unable to speak in his own defence, Billy retorts with a
blow which kills Claggart.

Billy and Claggart enact a conflict which Arendt portrays as one between "goodness beyond virtue and evil beyond vice."[7] For her, virtue and vice are legitimate human phenomena and no form of politics is devoid of either. Indeed, Arendt recognizes virtues and vices as moral categories compatible with normal human relationships. The opposite is true of absolute goodness (goodness beyond virtue) and absolute evil (evil beyond vice): both are perpetually at war with this world. They are phenomena which transcend the human bounds of human life lived among men. They bespeak a world of saints and devils, not of human beings with foibles and strengths.

Arendt's conviction that absolute goodness can be dangerous is bound to seem painfully incongruous since it controverts the common-sense understanding of goodness. Arendt maintains, however, that absolute goodness is the same as morality properly understood: it is rigid, exacting and uncompromising, and the crucial point about this calibre of goodness is that it "can only act violently"[8] when confronted with untruth and deception. Billy Budd is an exemplary instance of such morality, a genuinely good man. Claggart and his lying progeny are utterly beyond his moral sensibility.

In Billy's case there is no doubt that he is innocent and that he has been falsely accused. But in the everyday world, the claim to absolute goodness and innocence cannot be established with such facility. In the public realm, particularly, absolute goodness is not easily discovered and is vouched for, if at all, only with great difficulty. Yet absolute goodness, convinced of the superior truth of its claim, will act with violence to right perceived wrongs. From the point of view of the shared world of politics, absolute goodness cannot but destroy the basis of shared life, which is primarily lived in speech and conversation and in a milieu characterized by "fundamental relativity."[9] Violence is anti-political because it does not respect the life of speech and the plurality of competing opinions. Violence seeks to master a competitive situation by coercively enforcing one opinion and silencing all others. For Arendt it is finally irrelevant whether the source of violence is absolute goodness or something else. In all circumstances violence in the realm of politics, justified or not, negates politics. Though she holds this view firmly, it does not prevent her from observing "that under certain circumstances violence—acting without argument or speech and without counting the consequences—is the only way to set the scales of justice right again."[10] These "certain circumstances" are and ought to be unusual and treated as such: the public realm cannot survive regular irruptions of violence.

Billy Budd is the archetype of the moral self in conflict with a world which is not and cannot be moral in his sense. His absolute goodness is the morality of man in the abstract, the morality of a figure who has no connections, at any level, with other men and their limited concerns. Billy is moral in the way he is because he is a private man who is in but not of this world. Thus he neither understands nor respects the conventions of this world and the tenebrous web of self-interest which characterizes human relationships. In other words, Billy's problem is that he is a self who is *self-less* and therefore he is absolutely and shockingly good.

Such a pure nature cannot but disregard rules and laws which are and aspire to far less than the perfect moral ideal. This is the root of Billy's troubles: his moral nature is unsuited for the common world of politics in which all of us are obliged to live. His moral nature is opposed to the rule of law which does not proscribe lies and deceit *a priori*. In Aristotelian terms Billy is the good man who insists on being good always and expects the political association as well to be always good. The latter expectation is illegitimate in that it seeks to establish the rule of moral perfection in a sphere not suited to such demands. As Arendt says, "the law, moving between crime and virtue cannot recognize what is beyond it."[11] Billy's action appeals for support from something beyond the Rule of Law and therefore beyond politics. The law, however, can only recognize Billy as a citizen and judge him as a citizen, not as a good and moral man.

The vocation of citizenship entails respect for the principles of constitutionalism. Billy Budd and Socrates were in this view guilty before the law and rightfully punished: it is pertinent to note that in their different ways both Billy Budd and Socrates accepted the verdict of the law. And they did so because they recognized that a civilized society requires a measure of stability, legality and regularity; that a moral community cannot exist if citizens disobey and violate the rule of law on moral grounds. For the morality of absolute goodness, argues Arendt, is the morality of private judgement, the "abstract morality" of the individual removed from the common realm of human affairs.[12]

This is indeed the paradoxical nature of morality properly understood: when it strays outside its legitimate sphere it inevitably becomes tyrannical and dangerous because its only concern is the integrity of its own self, not the shared community, not the common world. Morality is suspicious of freedom and the realm of appearance, because they usually do not respect its imperious and exacting demands. If adhered to with conviction, morality in championing the commandments of the individual conscience is at best a mixed blessing in the realm of politics. In cases of blatant injustice, absolute morality will cast its vote on the side of right and goodness and thus invite approval of the community. But in cases where the conflict between good and evil is less clear cut, the result will be that "conscience will stand against conscience," the moral self against the community, and morality against the shared realm of politics.[13]

As Arendt understands it, the critical problem here is the fragility of the communal reality and the communal order which politics establishes. Morality, because of its primary interest in the self and its private reality, will inevitably undermine the basis of the shared reality and stability of politics which thrives on the ethic of compromise between a plurality of citizens. For politics, as Arendt never tires of insisting, is the order of freedom, action and public excellence. The rule of absolute moral norms cannot sanction a worldly reality which treats ordinary lies, minor deceptions, hypocrisy and hyperbole with mild disapprobation. It is in the nature of absolute morality to strongly condemn the moral ruses of worldly men and the morally lukewarm character of most human relationships.

Judged in terms of the crucial distinction between *vita activa* and *vita contemplativa* underscoring Arendt's political theory, absolute morality lies squarely in the domain of the latter. In this sphere alone can the idiom of life be an exclusively moral one, since this sphere is the locus of truth, goodness and perfect knowledge, appropriated independently of the public realm and public action. In contrast, the public realm is founded on a plurality of interests, opinions, temperaments and knowledge. Ironically, only on this basis can a polity exist as a moral community.

Though she judges Billy Budd by the strict standards of the public realm, she must know that no political community can survive without standards of moral justice. In fact Arendt is fully aware of this: there is no question in her mind that Billy's fatal blow against Claggart is morally just. From the viewpoint of politics, however, Captain Vere's death sentence against Billy is equally just—politically just. This is the heart of the issue: that in the shared public realm moral ideals and moral judgements are not at all irrelevant but they must take into account the public interest and the public world without which there would be no place to render justice, political or moral.

Undeniably there is considerable ethical risk involved in a theory which tacitly regards Claggart as more of a "citizen"—a public self—than Billy Budd. Though Arendt readily agrees with Melville's description of Claggart as "naturally depraved," her passionate commitment to the public realm and public freedom encourages her to ally herself, even if implicitly, with Claggart and against Billy Budd. Machiavelli's contrast between ethics and politics is not irrelevant to her view of Billy's predicament. In one sense, Arendt's interpretation is quite Machiavellian, siding as she does with Captain Vere's "correct" political judgement. But the Machiavellian analogy should not be pressed too far: Arendt neither doubts Billy's innocence and decency, nor the elemental justice of his stand against Claggart. If Billy failed the test of citizenship, Claggart failed far more decisively to measure up to her ideal of the public self.

For Arendt, nevertheless, the crucial point is that in the human condition, morality makes sense as part of a social order and its larger purposes. This is the unstated assumption of Arendt's political theory. Unsurprisingly, on this view, abstract absolute morality is as unintelligible as it is inapplicable in the public realm. To the objection that there is great moral danger in this view, Arendt would say that a true public realm would disallow deliberate immorality and injustice.

ROBESPIERRE

Billy Budd and Robespierre, as Arendt sees them, have this in common: they are absolute moral selves who pit themselves against the public realm in the name of absolute moral justice, Billy on his own behalf and Robespierre on behalf of the poor masses. In passing it is worth noting that an important difference exists between the context in which Arendt judges Billy and the one in which she judges Robespierre: the former is metaphorically public, the latter is actually public and political.

Arendt contends that an absolute morality, born of pity and compassion, usurped and dominated the public domain in France in 1789. For her this fact is central to understanding the French Revolution and its rapid descent into terror. She sees this event as a terrifying example of the tyrannical and destructive role of absolute morality in the realm of politics. Once again Arendt deploys her theory of the public realm in pressing her case against the Revolution. This is not to say that she opposed the occurrence of the Revolution and the inevitable violence. On the contrary. What distresses her is the success of the Revolution in subverting its deepest impulse and its sole justification: the founding of a true public realm, a true space of freedom. She takes this to be the *raison d'être* and the real meaning of revolution.[14] That she is horrified by the French reign of terror goes without saying.

The French Revolution began as a political action "against tyranny and oppression" but soon turned into a moral crusade "against exploitation and poverty" of the poor and the unfortunate.[15] The roots of this transformation were profoundly moral in the best sense. Robespierre and Saint-Just were deeply moved by the necessitous condition of the majority of Frenchmen. They sought in good conscience and in the proud manner of men offended by the moral injustice of the condition of poverty, to lend their hearts and power to liberating the poor "from suffering."[16] In their minds there were hardly any doubts about the absolute moral primacy of meeting the needs of the poor majority. They understood the main task of the Revolution to be not simply the founding of a free Republic, but the support of the interests of the poor and needy. Their limited political aims gave way to an ambitious moral design of the good and just society.

Arendt recognizes that pity for those who suffer ,from necessity and perennial poverty is a legitimate human feeling. But pity is too diffuse and limitless an emotion to serve as a platform of revolutionary action in politics, only because suffering is ubiquitous and protean in its manifestations. Yet this is precisely what Robespierre and his friends tried to accomplish through political means. Their motives were beyond reproach, but their grasp of the realities and the limitations of politics was poor. "Pity, taken as the spring of virtue," she writes, "has proved to possess a greater capacity for cruelty than cruelty itself."[17] That is, the political attempt to stamp out the cruelty of poverty has usually turned into a sharper form of cruelty against the whole of society. Indeed, according to Arendt, Robespierre's undeniable pity for the poor—the moral purity of his motives notwithstanding—issued into a bloody reign of terror to which some of the poor, the rich and many of the leaders succumbed as well.

The reasons for the terror are not hard to discover and they bear upon the nature of politics and of relationships within the community. In their conscious attempt to root out poverty and injustice, selflessness, honesty and pity for the unfortunate became the dominant moral virtues in the calculations of Robespierre and his companions. Purity of heart and a passionate hatred of hypocrisy emerged as the primary virtues of those who would fight against all manner of social injustice.[18] In this climate of opinion, Arendt maintains, it became essential not only to display one's virtues in public but to act in a manner which left no room for the merest suspicion about the goodness of one's motives. It was not enough to appear to be virtuous in the ordinary sense: one had to bare his private soul and his private thoughts to public scrutiny. In short, hypocrisy, the idiom of aristocratic life in France before 1789, became the greatest crime in the eyes of Robespierre and his fellow leaders.[19]

Behind the demand for baring the heart lay the moral injunction that the leaders of the revolution should be pure, innocent, and good human beings. In Arendt's view, however, human motives are naturally enmeshed in darkness and rarely known even to the actors themselves. The "search for motives" is doomed to "poison all human relations" because these motives can never be established with any degree of certainty.[20] To imagine otherwise is to doubt all motives and all men at all times. Under such conditions human relationships would lack the minimum measure of reality and predictability.

From the point of view of politics, Robespierre's demand that motives should be unquestionably moral denied the distinction between the private and the public, to the detriment of both realms. In Robespierre's terms there is no public self; only the private man who presents himself as such in the public realm. As a consequence, public ordeals of self-inspection and public protestations of honesty and purity of soul become necessary for all public actors. What thus appears in public is the naked self, indeed the moral self, who invites communal approval. But this is only ostensibly so because the suspicion of hypocrisy, of play-acting, can never be entirely eliminated. Since one does not and cannot trust completely the veracity and the authenticity of one's own motives, those of others are less likely to inspire confidence and trust. For Arendt it is inherent in the logic of this form of public exposure that it leads to charges of bad faith. In her own words, "Robespierre's insane lack of trust in others, even in his closest friends, sprang ultimately from his not so insane but quite normal suspicion of himself."[21]

In the public realm, as we have seen, public appearance constitutes reality, and the "lack of trust in others" necessarily undermines the political association as a moral community. This follows from the fact that the public self cannot be trusted precisely because the private self and private motives cannot be trusted. Since the public self is now seen as a faithful extension of the private self, its integrity is no longer presumed to be self-evident. On the contrary, this self has become part of the public domain and open to public scrutiny. Robespierre's demand that revolutionaries display their motives, that they should not be hypocrites, entailed an explicit attack on the very notion of politics in the ancient Greek sense, as the arena of the men who choose to present themselves as citizens, as public men. For Robespierre public men and private men became indistinguishable precisely because of the moral character of the problem at stake.

This problem was the fate of the poor and the unfortunate. To ameliorate and improve their condition required moral commitment first and foremost. And this commitment, according to Arendt, is in essence a private moral judgement about a private matter: the satisfaction of needs and wants. The ends of politics are freedom and action in the public space, not the management of economic demands. When Robespierre adopted the poor and placed their interests at the centre of politics, it was not freedom but morality and goodness which became the dominant characteristics of public business. Hence the private motives of public men became an issue, because the public good had become a moral good. In this ethical mood, insufficient sympathy for the cause of the poor was readily denounced as hypocritical and immoral.

Arendt contends that the intensity of moral fervour evidenced by Robespierre and his followers on behalf of the poor contained within it the seeds of great violence. Violence was intrinsically part of the nature of the problem—poverty—and it was inherent in the moral interpretation of the problem as an aspect of justice.[22] But its resolution would have been less violent, she seems to imply, if it had been kept out of the public realm. Once poverty became the first order of public action, violence and terror against those who for one reason or another did not totally endorse the cause of the poor became the rule of the revolution.

Thus the peculiar political significance of the French Revolution lies in its dual confusion of politics with the claims of nature, and of politics with the claims of morality. Robespierre launched a formidable attack on the idea and the ideal of politics when he made need and poverty a matter of justice in the public realm. Necessity and morality combined in the course of the Revolution to cast serious doubt on the worthiness of politics and the sense of worldliness in the life of men. For Robespierre politics had to justify itself before the bar of nature and the altar of absolute goodness, because only the latter were morally unspoiled, honest, "without hypocrisy."[23]

The morality of absolute goodness served to pervert politics and the idea of the public realm where men could assert their individual unique identities. The public or political self, as we have seen, is the antithesis of natural man: he is an unnatural self, an "artificial" self beyond nature. Such a self is no longer conceivable when nature or natural man is the ideal, as in Robespierre's revolutionary view. Unnatural man is a man with a mask of some sort which sets him apart from nature. Robespierre however hated all masks as statements of hypocrisy.

Arendt holds that the mask in theatre as in public life endows the individual with a *persona*—a distinct personality.[24] In all forms of truly human association relationships occur between persons with recognizable identities, not between natural selves. In politics in particular it is always the man with a *persona* who counts, who enjoys rights and performs duties. Citizenship is in one sense a concentrated expression and justification of legal personality and the rights which attach to it. In the human condition of *shared* life, the masks in which men appear in the public realm testify to the civilized nature of both the participants and the community. Those who do not so appear, like slaves, are politically and humanly "irrelevant being(s)."[25] As Arendt sees it, Europeans murdered Africans because they had no recognizable identities beyond the ones naturally given. And it was no accident that the Nazis removed all traces of individual uniqueness from their victims before murdering them *en masse*. In the modern world statelessness is a singularly relevant example of people without political masks and therefore without rights of any kind. Without masks, in short, human beings are in danger of losing their lives, let alone emerging as individuals with identifiable selves.

Morality of the kind represented by Robespierre is exclusively interested in the moral character of the public actors and in the indisputable truth of its own convictions. Arendt sees this kind of morality as an argument for privacy as distinct from an argument in favour of public life. Robespierre and his friends failed to understand that the human condition is a condition of plurality, and that it is inhospitable to the rigid moralism of single truths. Public life or politics thrives on debate, conversation and compromise, not on absolute truths, imagined or real. The dilemma is neatly captured in the "old Latin adage," "Let justice be done though the world may perish."[26] Justice, that is to say, may very well destroy the shared world of men and thus may condemn men to even greater rounds of injustice. Moral justice, which is contemptuous of the tenuous and compromised nature of worldly relationships, may lay the foundations of moral injustice in the long run. For Arendt, absolute morality may save souls and provide salve for troubled consciences, but it will destroy the very context in which justice may eventually be rendered.

So unusual is this account, that one is inclined to suspect Arendt of having taken leave of her senses. There is little here of the historical facts of the French Revolution and even less of elementary moral sympathy for both the victims of the *ancien régime* and the revolutionaries who fought against it. This account is in no sense an instance of historical scholarship. "Miss Arendt is, to put it mildly, no historian"[27] and her judgements are not based on such a claim. She thinks the revolution "ended in disaster"[28] because of a dual failure: that of the public sensibility to take root, and the philological failure to understand the meaning of revolution.

To deny that Arendt's view on this matter are factually and "morally troublesome"[29] would be absurd. Nor can it be denied that her strictures against the humanitarian ideals of Robespierre and his fellow revolutionaries evoke much of the negativism of Edmund Burke's stance on the French Revolution. Like Burke, Arendt nearly ignores the abject poverty, corruption and outright injustice which characterized life in the *ancien régime*. These are the facts which led to the Revolution, which spurred men of goodwill to seek a more just polity and society, not any abstract, disembodied passion for the concept of freedom. Revolutions have never been understood solely as attempts to lay the foundation of freedom. They have always been fought for the sake of freedom *and* justice, *and* happiness.

But it is crucial not to confuse Arendt's critique with the substance of Burke's philippic against the French Revolution. Burke's is an essentially religious attack on the revolution itself as an unnatural and arrogant challenge to the "entailed inheritance" of Frenchmen long vindicated by tradition. Burke saw the revolution as a "sacrilegious" offence against nature and providence.[30] By contrast, Arendt valorized the revolution as a deliberate invention for the sake of public freedom. Contrary to Burke, she lauded the Revolution as an attempt, against Nature, to found a "space of appearance" for free words and deeds. For Arendt, freedom and politics in her sense are possibilities that can be realized only if men are willing to challenge the natural and the inherited.

To judge by her source material,[31] Arendt was clearly not unaware of the basic injustices suffered by the majority of Frenchmen. She knew them and knew them well but she believed that Robespierre and his associates were wrong. Her unusual account should not be taken as an argument in favour of injustice, even less as a treatise in favour of immorality. For Arendt held firm to the belief that the absolute morality of the unworldly self is quintessentially private and hostile to freedom, action, and finally to the public realm and the public self. Ironically, it is in the name of the highest of human capacities that Arendt rails against absolute morality and justice in the public realm. For a political community uninterested in freedom, action and excellence would not only be unpolitical, it would be inhuman and immoral. This is the substance of her reasoning in rejecting the claims of absolute morality on the public realm.

EICHMANN

Unlike Billy Budd and Robespierre, Eichmann was a protagonist in a preternatural drama of evil: genocide against the European Jews. This contrast in context can hardly be overstressed. But even in this extraordinary context, there is a familiar element: the presence of a "moral" absolute—in Eichmann's case, an overriding commitment to himself and his private interest. Arendt's judgements about Eichmann and his Jewish victims make sense in terms of her political theory, specifically in terms of her critical distinction between the private and the public. Stated differently, it was from the viewpoint of politics in her sense that she made her critical judgements.

None of her critics has understood this. For that matter, none of her admiring defenders, as far as I know, has seen this either. The failure on the part of her detractors to take into account this crucial fact is the main reason for the ensuing misunderstanding. For the substance of the bitter controversy, provoked by her book and relevant in this context, was that she had judged, harshly judged, Jewish behaviour in face of the terror of the "final solution" as essentially immoral; that her account exonerated Eichmann because he was banal and condemned his victims for failing to fight back, indeed for co-operating with their killers.[32]

Though her judgement was certainly harsh, she did not even come close to condemning the "Jewish leaders"—only the leaders, not the Jewish people—by some absolute moral yardstick.[33] Indeed, Arendt subscribed to no such standard. Her critics misread her "public" judgement as an absolute moral judgement and then chose to read into it things which Arendt had never said. For instance, she never said that the victims were guilty of their own murder, that Eichmann was innocent, that the Jews should have fought back, that Justice was not done at Jerusalem. These charges are all false, yet they were routinely voiced at the height of the controversy.

Why was such misreading so rampant? The answer has to do with Arendt's audacity in raising questions about something which had long been considered canonical: the image of the Jew as victim. In the *Origins*, as early as page five, she had hinted at her dissatisfaction with arguments which presupposed the "perfect innocence" of victims of mass murder. Arendt was not persuaded by theories which completely "discharged" the victims of all "responsibility."[34] She did not say and did not mean that the victims were therefore guilty.

In *Eichmann*, she was far more vocal and far more specific in questioning the victim image. What seems to have cut deep is that she raised such questions in the context of the trial of a man responsible (with others) for the murder of millions of Jews. Challenging the victim image in this context was bound to cast doubt on the total innocence of the victims and the survivors. For, as Norman Fruchter has argued, in much stronger language, Arendt in effect "questioned the myth of the victim which Jews tend to substitute for their history" and which "guarantees [them] a unified identity."[35] Understandably, her simultaneous depiction of Eichmann as a banal mediocrity must have been too hard to bear with equanimity.

It is not necessary to accept Fruchter's characterization of the victim image as a "myth" to recognize the truth in his argument. Her critics' uniformly bitter and angry tone is otherwise puzzling and unintelligible. The following headline in the *Intermountain Jewish News* was a uniquely vulgar expression of this bitterness: "*Self-Hating Jewess Writes Pro-Eichmann Series.*"[36] But the same sentiment was also apparent in a Jewish scholar as serious and as learned as Gershom Scholem. In his letter to Arendt, he accused her of lacking "*Ahabath Israel*: 'Love of the Jewish people . . .' " and engaging in "a mockery of Zionism."[37] On the second point, Scholem was essentially right. What is intriguing about these criticisms, and this is only partly true of Scholem, is that they do not face up squarely to the questions raised by Arendt. Instead, her critics, on the one hand, deny her thesis and proceed to question her motives and, on the other, attempt to discredit her historical scholarship. Jacob Robinson's *And the Crooked Shall Be Made Straight: The Eichmann Trial, the Jewish Catastrophe, and Hannah Arendt's Narrative*[38] has yet to be equalled in its vigorous commitment to do the latter. Robinson uncovered numerous minor mistakes in dates, names, places, but in spite of his fastidious devotion to his task, he failed to undermine her thesis. Nor did he advance a counter-argument.[39]

Robinson's failure eloquently proves what should have been clear to him all along: that Arendt's thesis was neither an exercise in scholarship in contemporary Jewish history, nor was it based on such a claim. The basic historical fact essential to her thesis, that the *Judenrat* (council of Jewish leaders) had "co-operated" with the Nazi authorities in the area under Eichmann's jurisdiction, was never in dispute. Raul Hilberg's *The Destruction of the European Jews*[40] had already established this fact. In fact, Arendt relied on Hilberg's evidence to argue her case. But the substance of her case depended on her peculiar theoretical judgements. Few of her critics seemed able or inclined to understand this—the one exception who deserves mention is Norman Podhoretz. He was astute enough to see that the questions Arendt raised could not "be answered by scholarship."[41] But none of her critics understood the central role her antecedent theory of politics played in her judgements on Eichmann and the Jews. In the context of this study, the crucial part this theory played in her treatment of the Eichmann case must be understood.

Fundamental to Arendt's political theory is the distinction between the public and the private. The thesis I shall argue is that the capacity to commit evil is intimately related to the nature of shared public life, that is, to politics in the ancient sense. Public life characterized by an excessive and almost exclusive concern for the private self and its interests is a precondition of evil: it is a necessary though not a sufficient condition. Such public life is, in substance, private family life carried on in and through the public realm. Arendt herself does not argue this thesis but it is implicit in *Eichmann*, and it is in terms of this thesis that her judgements become intelligible.

Concern for and interest in the self is neither wrong nor undesirable in itself. Arendt deems self-interest to be moral in nature, in that it seeks to protect and preserve the self.[42] In this sense the morality of Eichmann's self-interestedness is not in doubt. The intensity of his self-concern is, however, deeply troubling, certainly from the viewpoint of absolute morality, Socratic and Christian, but also from the point of view of the political community. In the peculiar context of Hitler's Germany, Eichmann's morality of self-interest did lead to extreme evil.

To Arendt, the problem of Eichmann is the problem of thoughtless evil—the banality of the evil-doer. Her concern is with the blatant fact that Eichmann participated in mass murder. That is the "factual" phenomenon that preoccupies her, that suggests to her that such evil is best described as the dramatic absence of good.[43] What happened at Auschwitz and Treblinka was evil. The nature of this evil is such, Arendt contends, that it is safer to rely on politics in her sense, than on morality and human goodness to combat it. For, as she puts it, "The sad truth of the matter is that most evil is done by people who never made up their minds to be either bad or good."[44]

For Arendt, Eichmann's guilt in the murder of European Jews and other people is beyond doubt and beyond dispute. He willingly and efficiently transported millions to the laboratories of death and he must hang for his deeds. In her "private" sentence on Eichmann, she condemns him to death, even as she reminds us again that no punishment can do justice to his crime.[45] For the survivors, Eichmann's end is only the beginning: what manner of man was he? How could he despatch millions to their death without once doubting the propriety of his actions? What kind of society would allow, indeed encourage, him to send millions to horrible torture and certain death? To consider these questions is to begin to understand, in some small measure, the nightmare of totalitarianism and the hazy shape of evil. To understand is not to condone, excuse or forgive: it is, in the language of Aristotle, Hegel and Arendt, to reconcile ourselves to the reality of a world in which such things are possible. Without this "reconciliation," life in this world would become, almost literally, impossible.[46] Moral outrage can rarely sustain itself beyond the next round of hunger.

Adolf Karl Eichmann was obviously not a good man, if by good we mean a man motivated by strong concern for his fellow human beings. In this demanding and exacting sense of the word, few men are indeed good. Eichmann, however, was not a good man even in the minimal sense of the term. He was oblivious to the fate of his fellow men. Both the man and his deeds were unarguably devoid of goodness. Yet he could be compassionate, Arendt writes, within the macabre and deathly confines of Auschwitz.

Consider the case of Bertold Storfer, a representative of the Jewish community in Vienna, whom Eichmann had known in his official capacity, for six years. Storfer, it seems, had attempted to escape; he was caught and sent to Auschwitz. When Eichmann was informed by the camp commandant of Storfer's arrival, he went to Auschwitz to "help" his "friend." This help consisted of transferring Storfer from a labour gang to light duty on the gravel paths in the camp. During his trial, Eichmann related this incident with some degree of self-satisfaction. He was particularly concerned to stress that he had, as he described it, a "normal human encounter" with Storfer. By this he meant, how much he enjoyed seeing and talking to his old friend.[47]

Eichmann was not in the least embarrassed by this "normal, human encounter" in an extermination camp! For him, everything was quite normal. Jews and criminals were regularly sent to Auschwitz and that was all there was to it. Storfer had simply been unlucky and Eichmann had done all he could for his friend. Clearly, Eichmann remained unaware of the bizarre meaning of Auschwitz, although he knew full well what went on in this camp.[48] Arendt asserts that a man does not have to be a good man to recognize the evil of Auschwitz. Every man should be able to discern elemental evil, even if he is unable to stop it. That much we have a right to expect of all human beings. Was Eichmann, then, an *obviously* evil and immoral man? Was he of the same issue as Melville's Claggart, suffering from a "natural depravity"?

Arendt's considered judgement is morally shocking and disturbing: Eichmann, she suggests, was not an obviously evil man, nor was he completely destitute of moral sense. He was not a devilish fiend, a fanatic, or even a sadist who enjoyed sending people to the gas chamber. He did not even hate the Jews.[49] In fact, this man, responsible for "unspeakable horrors," was a pathetic, vacuous and ludicrous creature. In her own words: "everybody could see that this man was not a 'monster' but it was difficult indeed not to suspect that he was a clown."[50]

Intelligent men and women, including scholars who had reflected at length on the Holocaust, did not see in Eichmann a clown, but an evil monster, a clever liar, a Jew-hater and a calculating criminal.[51] But Arendt was not alone in her unusual evaluation of Eichmann's personality. François Bondy had depicted Eichmann in almost identical terms, soon after the trial. American philosopher Walter Kaufmann was struck by the "nauseous triviality" of this mass murderer; and the American poet Robert Lowell could not get away from the fact that Eichmann was an "appallingly uninteresting man."[52] For normal thinking men, it was the plain counsel of common sense which demanded that the criminal fit the crime. Eichmann had to be a monster, he had to be a devil of heroic proportions. Even for men like literary critic Harold Rosenberg, schooled in the moral ambiguities of human life, Eichmann was not only guilty of evil deeds, he was himself evil and he had intended to commit evil.[53] The sheer enormity of the crime silenced in such men measured moral judgement, which could conceivably be interpreted as less than total in its condemnation of the person of Eichmann.

By contrast, Arendt sought to "understand" what stared her in the face: the painful and dramatic incongruity between the trivial, banusic clown Eichmann and the immeasurable evil of his deeds.[54] What manner of man was he then? In many ways Eichmann was a remarkably normal man. So normal that Arendt describes him as "terribly and terrifyingly normal." At least one Israeli psychiatrist was appalled by his impeccably "normal" and indeed "desirable" attitude to family and friends.[55]

A not too bright son of a "solid middle-class family," Eichmann was plagued by recurring failure, that is, until he cast his lot with the Nazis. He failed to graduate from engineering school. He was fired from his job as a travelling salesman for the Vacuum Oil Co. in 1932. From his testimony at the trial, it became evident that as far as he himself, his family and his social class were concerned, he was already a failure. He had not acquired a career and there did not seem much chance of securing one in the future. What galled him most about his misfortune was his lack of respectability in the eyes of his peers, his lack of social status among members of his own class. In April 1932 he joined the party, as he had joined many other organizations, including the Y.M.C.A. He joined, Arendt convincingly contends, not out of any conviction, but in the spirit of a man who cannot think of anything better to do with his life. But he certainly did have a motive; he was an ambitious man in search of a career, in pursuit of advancement. The party seemed like the ideal channel for his mundane normal aspirations. In time he became the party expert on Jewish affairs and assumed responsibility for the transportation of Jews to concentration camps.

In the picture that Arendt paints in the barest of colours, Eichmann emerges as an outstandingly private man, obsessed with his career to an extraordinary degree. His sense of privacy did not entail any notion of solitary existence removed from the common world. Rather he was a private man in the sense that his entry into the public realm was motivated entirely by his desire to be a social and financial success. His ruling passions were "personal advancement" and the preservation of his self.[56] To achieve these aims, as his record clearly proves, he was prepared to do almost everything.

In a certain sense he was no different from the thousands of other men eager not only to survive but to become successful. Self-interest is without doubt a legitimate motive for human action. In the political history of the West, the rejection of self-interest is not a conspicious theme. Speculative political theory, at least since Aristotle, has also pre-supposed the legitimacy of self-interest in its ideal regimes. But not until the advent of the modern age did the doctrine of self-interest *in its own right* receive a philosophical defence and justification, as it did in the theory of Thomas Hobbes. His unsentimental depiction of the private man invites attention because of the peculiar nature of his self-interest. Hobbesian man, fearing for his life and jealous of his self, has no conception of public good independent of his private interest; he has no sense of responsibility towards his fellow men or towards the state, save insofar as such concern enhances his personal interest. In short, Hobbes' portrait is that of the classical bourgeois.[57] The idol and the ideal of bourgeois success cannot but silence the citizen, the public man.

The liberal philosophy of John Locke clearly sets much store by self-interest, individuality and privacy; its roots are undeniably Hobbesian. The Lockean liberal, however, is not the unrestrained bourgeois. For Locke the public realm and public good are worthy and necessary elements in the calculations of liberal men. Politics is not to be despised, even though self-interest may well undermine allegiance to the public realm and the common good. In Nazi Germany, it was the triumph of this self-interested privacy which pre-disposed men to systematically and routinely perpetrate perhaps the most unspeakable crime in human history. In this frame of judgement, Eichmann was the norm, not the exception. What distinguished him was his single-minded zealousness in making a total success of his career. But success eluded even the likes of Eichmann. To the end he never ceased to lament the fact that he had not advanced beyond the rank of lieutenant-colonel.

No doubt rising unemployment, poverty, social disintegration and general "superfluousness" combined with the bourgeois ethic of success to more or less ensure the primacy of private needs and private security. There were good social and economic reasons which led men to value career and advancement over public honour and dignity. Still, "nothing proved easier to destroy," writes Arendt, "than the privacy and private morality of people who thought of nothing else but safeguarding their private lives."[58] For it was not the sadists and the perverts who managed the complex machinery of genocide, but the ordinary job-holder and family man, whose only "vice" was an inordinate passion for survival and success.[59] This quotidian personality was so deeply and fatally engrossed in securing his private interests, that he saw a veritable dichotomy between the private and the public realms. Indeed the public realm did not exist for him except as the source of his occupation, as the vein of his private life.[60] These stirrings of self-interested privacy in themselves promised neither salvation nor doom. But when they were enlisted in the service of a dynamic and visionary statement of new politics, the result proved to be horribly tragic.

In her earlier work, the *Origins*, Arendt had argued that destruction of privacy was one of the essential elements of totalitarian rule. To now suggest that it was the triumph of privacy which encouraged totalitarian evil may seem contradictory: the contradiction is not a real one. Totalitarian rule certainly destroyed the traditional private person as a juridical and moral being capable of individual choice and judgement, and it destroyed as well the normal array of social and private groups to which individuals could freely belong. But in its place totalitarianism substituted the Movement, which provided both occupation and purpose to thousands of normal, decent men, hungry for jobs, careers and success. In other words, totalitarianism revived and elevated the private realm of needs, wants and security to the position of respectable public ambition, while at the same time eliminating the private moral space indispensable to every human life. In Nazi Germany, it was this self-interested privacy, founded on necessity and ambition, which flourished at the expense of the older private self. In terms of our tradition of political theory, totalitarianism resembles nothing so much as the celebration of the Hobbesian state of nature and its compelling demands.

It is this utter and abrasive normality of the likes of Eichmann which is so difficult to accept, yet is undeniable. Eichmann was impossible to visualize without his organization charts, his fussy stale speech, his bureaucratic pride or his sharpened pencils despatching trucks and trains of human beings to their death. In the words of François Bondy, Eichmann "must have seen blood in terms of paper." According to Arendt, nevertheless, Eichmann did have a conscience of sorts. But it was a conscience which did nothing to save Jews except once—an occasion which he did not remember; a conscience which revolted at the thought of any exceptions to the final solution as unjust and unfair, and which led him to ignore Himmler's order to stop sending Hungarian Jews to the death camps at the end of the war. Indeed, as Eichmann put it, he would have had a "bad conscience" only if he had ceased to do his job—that is, "ship millions" properly and efficiently to their doom. His conscience had fused with the murderous purpose of his job and it functioned as a conscience only with respect to his occupation and only within the assumed legitimacy of the "final solution."[61]

Eichmann's conscience is a travesty of what we normally mean by conscience. Arendt leaves no doubt about this. For her, however, although Eichmann was "perfectly incapable of telling right from wrong," he was not entirely devoid of a conscience.[62] This is indeed a perverse paradox. Eichmann hated liars, he despised those who took pleasure in maiming and torturing, and he could not stand the sight of blood. He was appalled at the idea of killing German Jews, but was boundlessly zealous in transporting other European Jews to extermination camps. He was a proudly law-abiding man, who knew the gist and meaning of Kant's categorical imperative, and he had lived by the precepts of duty and obedience. He did all he could to ensure that Jews on their way to the camps were not unnecessarily subjected to pain and discomfort. The uncomfortable fact of the matter, according to Arendt, is that these are admirable qualities in any man. In sum, he was a conscientious and nauseatingly courteous man who carried out his assigned functions with incredible pleasantness.

Eichmann's conscience, however, stopped short of questioning the final solution. The modesty of Eichmann's conscience in face of the organized genocide of the Jews raises difficult and crucial questions about the relationship between the moral impulse in man and political life: it is necessary to consider the nature of this relationship.

Mass murder is, strictly speaking, not a political but a moral problem: it is first of all a question of moral rightness or wrongness. This is the view to which Arendt adhered though not in terms that I have used. In the case of Nazism, politics subserved rather than initiated its main purpose—mass murder. Politics came into play after this purpose had been defined and decided. This is where the difficulty about Eichmann's conduct presses itself most sharply. The good man will necessarily query any command to murder or effect the murder of an individual or a group—murder means the killing of the innocent. In politics it is not the good man but the citizen who takes part as ruler or as subject. The citizen may or may not be a good man. Citizenship does not require nor does it necessarily entail the use of the moral faculty, although the presumption that the citizen is also a moral being is not therefore illegitimate. In fact that presumption is logically entailed in our definition of the "good citizen." To the extent that the citizen exercises his moral judgement, he does so as a private individual, not as a citizen: because moral judgement is a private matter between a man and his conscience. To this view Arendt held fast. In politics the appeal to conscience cannot be accepted as justifiable ground for refusal to obey orders, simply because the claims of conscience can be as varied and subjective as the number of individuals in society. No political order can survive perennial disobedience based on conscience. In part, this was the predicament of Socrates and of the conscientious objectors to the war in Vietnam.

Arendt insists that conscience is as a rule inappropriate in the realm of politics, particularly since political action necessarily involves harmful consequences.[63] To participate in politics is invariably to dirty one's hands. In these terms Eichmann cannot be faulted. He was undoubtedly a model "citizen" of the Third Reich. In fact he was overly conscientious in the pursuit of his murderous duties. His inverted morality led him to do his best to execute the final solution. His conscience made it possible for him to do precisely what was most criminal.

As I read Arendt, Eichmann's criminal conduct was not due to a failure of conscience, but due to his inability to realize that he was not participating in normal politics. This is crucially important to understand. As a citizen, Eichmann could not reasonably have been expected to consult his conscience. But he did and his conscience did not stop him, even though he was not an *obviously* evil man and he did not *intend* to kill the Jews. This is certainly hard to accept. If Eichmann had a conscience, how could he possibly not have recognized the wrongness of his actions? Arendt's answer is radically new and important. Conscience, she reasons, is a private matter, *but* it does not function independently of the world. Conscience is another name for the individual meditation on the moral rightness or wrongness of human action in the world. In this basic and rarely noticed sense, conscience is tied to the public world. Eichmann's problem was that he found no one, absolutely no one, "who actually was against the final solution."[64] No one among his peers and no one in Germany, as far as he knew, was opposed to the final solution. The critical point here is that, if Eichmann had any doubts about mass murder, they disappeared in the complete absence of dissenting voices. Eichmann's conscience functioned perfectly well in the peculiar world of the Nazis. It was not Eichmann's conscience *per se* which failed him, it was the conscience of the good and respectable society around him. This society "reacted" exactly as he did to the final solution. Who, after all, was Eichmann to presume that he was right and they were wrong?

This collective failure of conscience points to a political problem of the first order. In Nazi Germany the public arena was not a political arena. This is an elusive but fundamental distinction. In Arendt's theory only those forms of public life are political which allow and encourage citizens to establish human relationships that transcend the kind of obligatory intercourse which the necessitous nature of men imposes upon them. True politics requires attentive citizens and friends in charge of public life, not the utilitarian calculations of the *homo economicus*.

The public realm in Nazi Germany was not a political realm at all: its characteristic passions were personal careers and racial-biological questions. Nazi politics was not centred on issues of communal concern—on the manner, the tone and the fate of the public life of citizens in the ancient Greek sense—but exclusively on private concerns. Among the Nazis and their supporters, there were no citizens, strictly speaking, with love and concern for the *polis*, the *res publica*, only private men in search of careers. To them, the public realm was no more than an organized and civilized market for jobs, promotion and success. For many of them, Hitler must have been the very model of a successful man—from painter to Führer—as he was for Eichmann.

In Nazi Germany, we witness the cruel triumph of an abnormal form of politics; a form of politics which throve on the desire of the ordinary man for personal success, on his limitless ambition to make good; a form of politics, furthermore, which linked itself to a vision of teutonic mastery nourished by the myth of Germany's racial destiny. The "citizen" of the Third Reich understood only the connection between his career and Hitler's version of Germany's historical task. What he did in the public realm mattered only in terms of his career and its significance in the scheme of the universal aspirations of the Third Reich. Public life under Nazi hegemony was neither public in its true purpose nor shared in a significant manner. In substance, Nazism, while maintaining its elaborate public image, privatized public life to the point of almost destroying it. Nazism recast the relationship between the private and the public realm in a manner which deprived the latter of its normal attributes of civility and humanity; instead the public realm was used to kill the moral and the human spirit in man and in his relationships with his fellow-men.

In the public realm, thus construed, inheres a moral fellow-feeling unique to the citizens who share their lives and concerns together. The distinction which Arendt draws between morality and politics is an argument specifically against the ethic of moral improvement and moral betterment as ultimate goals of political action; it is not an argument against the natural flow of protective friendships and mutual concern which does and should characterize true political life.

On this view, it is the public-political realm that defines the limits of what is permissible in the common life of men, that serves as a barrier to public evil.[65] Hence a particular kind of public morality and moral judgement is intrinsic to the public realm in so far as the latter harbours a community of citizens. The fate of the Jews and other people ought to have been a *political* issue in the *public* realm. In the absence of this realm in Nazi Germany, evil in the person of Eichmann and his cohorts flourished unchecked. This is the essential thrust of Arendt's unargued argument.

The tragedy of the Holocaust can thus be traced, in large part, to the failure of most Germans and the civilized world to acknowledge the profoundly anti-political nature of Nazi politics. According to Arendt, Jews no less than Germans were disposed to see the Third Reich as no more than a more radical version of normal politics. They did not seem to understand that the Nazis were determined not "to share the earth"[66] with other races. Many Jews falsely assumed that Nazism was simply a more virulent form of anti-semitism, which would pass as similar outbreaks had done in the past. They had no reason to imagine the worst because the worst was unimaginable.

Nevertheless Arendt is sharply critical of the Jewish *leadership* for not refusing to co-operate with the Nazis, in selecting fellow-Jews for "resettlement" in concentration camps elsewhere.[67] Her point is that even if the leaders did not know the fate that was to befall their people, they should not in any event have co-operated at all with the Nazis. Since she had, contrary to widespread misreading, never asked and in fact had dismissed the question, Why did they not revolt? as "cruel and silly,"[68] what should they have done? There was, she writes, "no possibility of resistance, but there existed the possibility of *doing nothing*," of "non-participation."[69] This harsh judgement still retains its truth against all the arguments that can be readily adduced to show how impossibly difficult the circumstances were in which choices had to be made. For it is a judgement about the failure of the public sensibility among the Jewish leaders.

The conclusion that Arendt drew from this failure was that:

if the Jewish people had really been unorganized and leaderless, there would have been chaos and plenty of misery but the total number of victims would hardly have been between four and a half and six million people.[70]

In a sense this conclusion, as Mary McCarthy has said, is "almost self-evidently true."[71] Then again it may not be true, knowing as we do that the Nazis were irrational enough to devote the required manpower and resources to meet their objective. What is clear, however, is that even as late as May 1944, when no Jewish leader could plead ignorance about the meaning of "resettlement," the Central Jewish Council of Hungary, in a letter to the Minister of Interior Andor Jarosz seeking an audience with him, could still say that

we do not seek the audience to lodge complaints about the merits of the measures adopted, but merely to ask that they be carried out in a humane spirit.

Richard L. Rubenstein, who cites this passage in his book *The Cunning of History*, is even harsher than Arendt in his judgement. He asserts that "it demonstrates that it made no difference whether a Jewish community knew of the fate that awaited them or not."[72] This is too categorical but it is hard not to agree with the assumption underpinning Rubenstein's judgement.

From the victims' side, the second crucially relevant factor in the tragedy of the Holocaust was their sense of privacy and private well-being. In the main the Jews were, like other people, occupied with their private careers, businesses and interests—in conditions which were far from normal. Yet very few chose to leave; the majority stayed for the sake of their private concerns and private accomplishments. "How could we leave? It would have meant giving up our homes, our work, our sources of income."[73] This summary of the reasons for not leaving eloquently captures the attitude and the problem of privacy. For Arendt, this *understandable* attachment to self-interested privacy contributed in some measure to the tragedy from the side of the victims as well.[74] Instead of acknowledging the new reality, many Jews withdrew deeper into privacy, though it must be stressed that this withdrawal was also a retreat into the spiritual shelter of the Jewish faith. Few people in this climate seemed to notice the collapsing horizon of normality.

The standard Arendt uses in judging Jewish conduct is not abstractly moral but political. She deplores the failure of the public sensibility: the failure to act as public selves in the minimum sense, to be alive to their public fate. For the leaders who ought to have known better, she reserves her strident contempt; for the Jewish people, caught between the Nazis and their leaders, she has genuine sympathy. The much-maligned "heartlessness" of her judgement also has another source: this is her conviction that "politics is not like the nursery; in politics obedience and support are the same."[75] For the Jewish leaders not to have known this is in Arendt's eyes neither understandable nor excusable.

To forestall misunderstanding, it must be stressed that the combined failure of conscience and of the public-political realm in Germany does not at all excuse Eichmann and his deeds. Nor does Arendt imply that it does. No political order, no matter how perverse, conditions its citizens totally and Eichmann must be presumed to have been free to reject the final solution. Indeed he was tried and held responsible on the basis of the legitimate juridical and moral presumption that he could have said no to evil. Arendt rightly says that when the normal world has fallen apart, we still have the right to expect the individual to think for himself and freely resist evil against all odds.

From the standpoint of politics, however, Eichmann's culpability is much less clear: he was certainly guilty but not in any obvious political or legal sense. He was faithful to both Nazi politics and Nazi legality. The moral context, however, in which he found himself was weak and undemanding: the Nazis had dispatched the maxims of Judeo-Christian morality into oblivion. There were no countervailing moral maxims available;

that is, there were no public and external standards to which one could appeal. It is her awareness of this fact which lends Arendt's discussion of Eichmann and his crimes a measure of defiant ambivalence. For in such a situation to hope for moral propriety, to fall back on morally abstract injunctions, is both foolhardy and dangerous.

As Arendt sees it, it is more realistic and more legitimate to expect to check public evil by appealing to the morality of shared citizenship. A commonly shared and prized public realm, housing a community of citizens concerned with each other's fate, may be the only real answer to the thoughtless commission of public evil by the likes of Eichmann.[76]

Though he failed ultimately as a *human* being, Eichmann failed also as a public citizen, as a member of the realm of plurality. This is why in her "private" sentence Arendt condemns him to death on the ground of her theory of politics: he must hang for "not wanting to share the earth with the Jewish people."[77] Even those who sympathized with her thesis on Eichmann failed to understand the reasoning behind this judgement because they did not know her political theory.[78] This and no other is the only moral "absolute" in her thought: that we *ought* to share the world with other people.

But clearly this standard is pitifully inadequate: it can be easily satisfied even in concentration camps as long as the inmates are kept alive. Arendt would of course condone nothing of the sort, but her position seems logically to commit her to this view. She seems not to have noticed, as well, that sharing the earth with the blacks is precisely what the imperial agents in Africa declined to do. She did not think the worse of those mass murders because the blacks had not fulfilled her conditions of humanity. This inconsistency is deplorable but her attitude towards blacks and other "unpolitical" people is quite consistent with her theory of politics.

To understand Arendt's strictures against self-interested privacy and absolute morality, is to understand that a peculiar kind of moral and prudential judgement supports and protects those who live and share in the public realm: it is not to deny the morality of self-interest or to imagine that no form of public life will give rise to evil. The knowledge that the capacity to commit evil may find sanctuary in the abodes of self-interested privacy may enable us to temper its excesses if not to prevent it. In the darkest of times, when all else falls apart, the public realm and the public selves may serve as the true moral community. That at least was her hope.

Hannah Arendt's political theory is best understood as a theory of public sensibility. Undoubtedly public life is materially based but it cannot become substantively public unless the sensibility which informs the citizens is truly public in spirit. In an important sense it is not necessary that the citizen should be a man of leisure and property. So long as his disposition is neither crassly necessitous nor utilitarian, he can be and act as a public self and indeed as a moral self, in the company of his fellow citizens. In the final analysis, it is the public sensibility that makes it possible to found and sustain the public realm, to check the irruption of evil, to nourish concern for the fate of fellow-citizens, and to encourage the exercise of freedom and the pursuit of human excellence in the shared "space of appearance."

As a political theorist, Arendt's greatest achievement was to recover and restore the ancient conception of public virtues and the public sensibility as part of the public realm. For men in the shared human condition, the public realm is the highest form of human association. To recognize this truth in an age entirely persuaded that privacy, private interests, and the private sensibility are the highest of human goods, is to rediscover the humanity and morality of political community and of citizenship. That Arendt has no positive doctrine of justice is her fundamental weakness. For no form of public life is worthwhile without a conception of justice. Though she neither intends to say, nor says, that justice is irrelevant in public life, her lack of interest in the subject is distressing. The question at issue is whether her theory unintentionally licenses injustice since her justification of ideal public life studiously disregards motives and consequences, the claims of moral justice. Still, this fact should be judged in the context of her crucial thesis that public life in the public realm generates its own peculiar and protective moral fellowship among citizens: *zoon politikon*, as Aristotle and Arendt knew, is blessed with the power of speech, the faculty of reason *and* the capacity to be just.

The limitations of her theory are real but her achievement is no less real: no one, not even Aristotle, has taught us to understand the intrinsic human and moral worth of the public realm and what it means to a public self, with as much noble passion and intelligence as Hannah Arendt. Her political theory is an astonishingly eloquent and sustained testimonial to the joys and the dangers of true public life.

NOTES

1 *Politics* (Oxford, 1946), 1276b-1277a.
2 *CR*: 61-62.

3 *HC*: 218-223; *REV*: 27.

4 *HC*: 177.

5 *BPF*: 245.

6 *REV*: 77.

7 Ibid.: 78.

8 Ibid.: 79.

9 *MDT*: 27.

10 *VLE*: 64.

11 *REV*: 79; cf. also 81.

12 *CR*: 90.

13 Ibid.: 64; see also *BPF*: 228, 245.

14 *REV*, Ch. I, especially 21-22.

15 Ibid.: 68, 70, 75, *passim*.

16 Ibid.: 107.

17 Ibid.: 85.

18 Ibid.: 91 and 92.

19 Arendt's treatment of Robespierre bears a striking similarity to Camus' critique of Saint-Just's "virtuous" demands; cf. *The Rebel* (New York, 1956): 121-132. She does not mention Camus in this context.

20 *REV*: 93.

21 Ibid.: 92.

22 Ibid.: 86, 108.

23 *REV*: 106; cf. 102-105.

24 Ibid.: 102.

25 Ibid.: 103.

26 Quoted by Arendt, *BPF*: 228.

27 George Lichtheim, "Two Revolutions," in *The Concept of Ideology* (New York, 1967): 119.

28 *REV*: 49.

29 George Kateb, *Hannah Arendt: Conscience, Politics, Evil* (Oxford, 1984): 29.

30 For a brief and very perceptive discussion of Burke's attitude, see J. M. Cameron, "Burke" in *Western Political Philosophers*, ed. Maurice Cranston (London, 1964).

31 *REV*: 100-102, 328-336.

32 Marie Syrkin, "Hannah Arendt: The Clothes of the Empress," *Dissent* 10, 4 (1963): 344-352; Lionel Abel, "The Aesthetics of Evil," *Partisan Review* 30, 3 (1963): 211-230; Gertrude Ezorsky, "Hanna Arendt Against the Facts," *New Politics* 2, 4 (1963): 53-73; Norman Podhoretz, "Hannah Arendt on Eichmann: A Study in the Perversity of Brilliance," in *Doings and Undoings* (New York, 1964): 335-353; Gershom Scholem in his letter to Arendt reprinted in *JEW*: 240-245. This is also the view of Stephen J. Whitfield in *Into the Dark: Hannah Arendt and Totalitarianism* (Philadelphia, 1980), Chs. 6-7. For an insightful discussion on the controversy, see Elisabeth Young-Bruehl, *Hannah Arendt: For Love of the World* (New Haven, 1982), Ch. 8.

33 *EIJ*: 118-125.

34 *OR*: 5-7.

35 "Arendt's Eichmann and Jewish Identity," in *For a New America*, ed. James Weinstein and David W. Eakins (New York, 1970): 424-425.

36 April 12, 1963.

37 *JEW*: 241, 245; for Arendt's view see "Zionism Reconsidered," in *JEW*: 131-163.

38 (New York, 1965).

39 See Walter Laqueur's favourable review in *JEW*: 252-259. For all his admiration for

Robinson's book, he felt compelled to say that Robinson never confronts the substantive issues.

40 (Chicago, 1961).

41 Norman Podhoretz, "Hannah Arendt on Eichmann," *op. cit.*: 337.

42 *CR*: 64; *HC*: 63; *OR*: 336.

43 *EIJ*: 252, 287; Hannah Arendt, "Thinking and Moral Considerations: A Lecture," *Social Research* (Autumn 1971): 417-446.

44 Ibid.: 438.

45 *HC*: 217; *EIJ*: 279.

46 *BPF*: 45.

47 *EIJ*: 50-51.

48 Ibid.: 50-51.

49 Ibid.: 26, 30.

50 Ibid.: 54.

51 In essence, this is the view shared, among others, by Marie Syrkin, Gershom Scholem, Lionel Abel and Gertrude Ezorsky. See footnote 32 above.

52 "On Misunderstanding Eichmann," in *Encounter* (Nov. 1961): 32-37; *Tragedy and Philosophy* (New York, 1969): 383; *New York Review of Books* (May 13, 1976): 6, respectively.

53 *Act and the Actor* (New York, 1970): 170-197.

54 Bruno Bettelheim was also struck by this incongruity and he agreed with the substance of her thesis. See his *Surviving* (New York, 1980): 258-273.

55 *EIJ*: 276.

56 Ibid.: 287.

57 See Arendt's concentrated and arresting analysis of the real nature of Hobbes' political theory in *OR*: 139-147.

58 *OR*: 338.

59 *CR*: 71 (fn. 35).

60 Arendt, "Organised Guilt and Universal Responsibility," in *Guilt: Man and Society*, ed. Roger W. Smith (New York, 1971): 255-267.

61 *EIJ*: 25.

62 Ibid.: 26.

63 *CR*: 60, 64, 84, 92.

64 *EIJ*: 116.

65 This view is implicit in her thought. For example, see *OR*: 316, 350-353, 437-452; *HC*: Chs. 24, 26, *passim*.

66 *EIJ*: 279.

67 Ibid.: 125, *passim*.

68 Ibid.: 11-12; also 283; *JEW*: 260-261.

69 *JEW*: 248-249.

70 *EIJ*: 125.

71 "The Hue and Cry," in *The Writing on the Wall* (New York, 1970): 59.

72 (New York, 1978): 70.

73 Bruno Bettelheim, "The Ignored Lesson of Anne Frank," in *Surviving*: 254.

74 This theme runs right through *EIJ*; see also *JEW*: 232-234; *OR*: 338.

75 *EIJ*: 279.

76 This view is also to be found in *REV*: 27, 256-257.

77 *EIJ*: 279.

78 For example, Daniel Bell, "The Alphabet of Justice," *Partisan Review* 30 (1963): 428-429; Dwight Macdonald in his letter, *Partisan Review* 31 (1964): 267.

Appendix

THE LIFE OF THE MIND

Since the posthumous publication of Arendt's *The Life of the Mind*, its relevance to her political theory has inevitably become a pressing question: whether the *Life* enhances in any significant way our understanding of her political theory, and whether it necessitates a serious re-evaluation of this theory. The answer to both questions is negative: the *Life* at best is unequivocally marginal and in fact irrelevant to her political theory. That is not to say that the *Life* eschews comment on politics but that its essential thrust is philosophical: this puts the *Life* squarely outside the public-political realm. Freedom and action, the true subjects of Arendt's political theory, are not mindless, but the elements of mind and thought evident in political life have the most tenuous relation to the concerns of the *vita contemplativa* (life of the mind).

From its self-conscious beginning in *The Human Condition*, Arendt's political theory presupposed a sharp distinction between the *vita contemplativa* and the *vita activa*. She maintained that these were separate and distinct vocations enjoined to different principles and impulses. The matter-of-course subsumption of the life of action to the *vita contemplativa* was the reason why political theory was stillborn, the fateful consequence of the assumed priority of the life of the mind over that of action. In her writings Arendt attempted, over a period of thirty years, to reverse this consequence. The strength of her conviction can be measured by the fact that she did no more than occasionally glance at the realm of the mind in a book devoted to the human condition. For her, the human condition was constituted by the plurality of men and their relationships. The solitary life of the mind was "out of order" in this *shared* condition. Arendt did not waver from this position even when she realized that there was a crucial link between the capacity to commit evil and the sheer inability to think, as in the case of a mass murderer like Eichmann. For she was forced to conclude

---

Notes to the Appendix appear on page 146.

142

that in the normal course of events, or even in emergencies, human beings rarely engaged in thinking. This was the harsh factual truth. Those who refused to succumb to the Nazi train of mass murder were something more than thinking human beings: they were good and decent men because only such men are distressed by bad conscience and evil deeds. For the rest, even if they engage in thinking, there is no necessary connection between thoughtfulness and the disinclination to do evil.[1]

For political actors caught in the thrust and parry of action in the public realm, there is no felt need to stop and think. This is the thesis of Arendt's essay on "Thinking and Moral Considerations," which tries to understand and account for the horrible evil Eichmann realized in the course of his official duty.[2] Arendt's thoughts on politics and morality, thinking and evil, conscience and goodness, served as the starting point for the highly personal reflections which became *The Life of the Mind*. This fact notwithstanding, the *Life* is a discourse on non-political matters: thinking and willing and associated activities of Mind. Unsurprisingly, certain themes familiar from her earlier writings reappear in the *Life* but their treatment here has no significant bearing on her political theory. To read the *Life* as if it were part of her political theory is to profoundly misunderstand her. Arendt did not intend the *Life* to be pressed into political service. Nor does what she says in the *Life* remotely warrant such an approach.

Having acknowledged that it was the puzzle of Eichmann's murderous behaviour which led her to consider the life of the mind, she could still say to Hans Jonas: "I have done my bit in politics . . . no more of that; from now on, and for what is left, I will deal with *transpolitical* things."[3]

Arendt was not being disingenuous. In summary terms, thinking and willing, as she understood them, are human faculties which presuppose withdrawal from the world, from the presence of other men, and cessation of all activity. These are isolated, *private* mental capacities exercised in solitude. Thinking is the dialogue man conducts with himself in the hope of capturing meaning and perhaps truth. It can clarify intention, unravel motive, and evaluate aim in the larger scheme of things when man meditates on his own. But it yields no results, no goals since it is its nature to turn and turn again upon itself.[4] Willing, by contrast, is more aggressive, more assertive and certain of itself in the course of the mental play which precedes action. If thinking is important in propelling action, willing is the preliminary spring to all action. Willing is therefore much closer to action, but its affinity to action in the final analysis proves to be apocryphal. Once begun, action has little use for thinking or willing.[5]

This is the gist of the faculties of thinking and willing, although Arendt avoids a precise definition of either faculty. What is clear, however, that both thinking and willing in their pure form are fundamentally anti-political—and in a less stringent understanding, pre-political. Thinking and willing articulate together or separately a way of life inimical to the intellectual chaos, the practical confusion and the moral anomalies characteristic of political life and worldly relationships. In various ways, thinking and willing require a strict order in men and in the world, an order responsive to assertions of the will and to reason's desire to impose and elicit rational meaning. The life of the mind necessarily subverts the seminal impulse and the principle of freedom at the heart of the *vita activa*: it cannot do otherwise and still be the life of the mind. But if it succeeds, the life of politics and action loses both its legitimacy and its *raison d'être* as a distinctively free and human way of life. According to Arendt this was precisely the fate that political theory and politics had to endure since Plato subsumed action to the interdictory claims of the mind.

In this context, the remarks of certain commentators merit notice. In a finely intelligent review, Sheldon Wolin concludes that the *Life* is essentially irrelevant to Arendt's political theory, although he does feel that the *Life* can be described as delineating a "politics of the mind."[6] Wolin means that like many of her earlier writings, the *Life* seeks to challenge and overturn entrenched conceptions, to loosen and unhinge the accumulated authority and power of these conceptions on the minds of thoughtful men engaged in understanding the mental realm.

Writing on the *Life*, philosopher Bernard Elevitch took strong exception to Wolin's use of the term "politics" in connection with this work. He felt that this term was entirely inappropriate and mistaken, and fraught with implications which *The Life of the Mind* did not authorize and could not sustain in view of its explicit concern with "transpolitical" things. Elevitch somewhat overstates his criticism of Wolin's carefully circumscribed use of the term "politics" but his central point is valid: the *Life* is not about politics or political theory.[7] Wolin would not quarrel with this assessment.

In a recent essay, Jean Yarbrough and Peter Stern critically address the relationship between Arendt's *Life* and her political theory.[8] Yarbrough and Stern engage the *Life* in a steady and diligent manner, elucidating, analyzing, and cautiously criticizing Arendt's thinking on the matters at hand. They try to be faithful to the spirit and the letter of the *Life* and in the main they succeed admirably. Ironically, their honesty and their fidelity to the thematic and intellectual content of the *Life* effectively undermine their proposed thesis: they fail to uncover or discover "political thought" in *The Life of the Mind*. Their failure was predictable because they knew well enough that the *Life* was an exercise in "pure philosophy."[9] Unintentionally, Yarbrough and Stern provide solid evidence against any serious claim that the *Life* is a work of political imagination or that it harbours rudiments of a political theory.

Arendt's intellectual scope was so wide, and her tendency to link apparently disparate themes so pronounced, that it often seemed that there was an intimate connection between *all* of her writings. Such a connection is indeed evident in the recurrence of certain large themes in many of her writings, but it is a mistake to assume such linkage without heeding her stated intention or the context. Lesser minds than Yarbrough and Stern will no doubt succumb to this illusion, to the detriment of both her political theory and her pure philosophy of the mind.

The *Life* is a challenging and profoundly serious work[10] but it has no bearing on Arendt's political theory. There remains one crucial question to consider: the political status of the faculty of judging which Arendt described as "the most political of men's mental abilities."[11] That she genuinely believed this cannot be doubted. She first touched on this issue in her 1960 essay "The Crisis in Culture." There she asserted that Kant in his *Critique of Judgement* had discovered the new faculty of judgement which implied "a political rather than a merely theoretical activity," in that judgement, unlike thinking and willing, presupposed the presence of others, specifically actors, and their "potential agreement" with each other.[12] For her, the issue became an urgent one because of Eichmann's astounding failure to make any judgements at all about the mass murder of fellow human beings. In view of her strong feeling about the crucial relevance of judging to politics, it is altogether remarkable that she did not postulate a theory of judgement in politics, in the fifteen years since she first asserted its importance.

One will of course never know why Arendt waited so long to tackle the question of judgement: until the moment of her death, in fact. But it seems to me that she hesitated and procrastinated because she did not really know the deeper sense in which judging was a political faculty. To say this is not to be unduly harsh or to say something without warrant. Her extant remarks on judging and judgement, including excerpts from her lectures on Kant's political philosophy,[13] propose no theory of judgement; indeed there is no sustained argument to be found in these suggestive fragments. Furthermore, it is very hard to see how her view of judging and judgement can be construed as political when it is the spectator, not the actor, who is in a position to judge and judge after the event. Judging entails detachment and distance from the scene of action. The person who judges cannot simultaneously be a participant. This expectation serves to deny the political actor the capacity to judge in the process of action, thus removing the faculty of judgement from the realm of politics.[14]

Judging and judgement fall to the spectator because judging entails thinking. The thinking involved in judging is not the same as thinking for the sake of meaning, but even in this diminished capacity it is still thinking, in this case "thinking the particular."[15] In the final analysis Arendt failed to find room for judging and judgement in the impatient and impassioned public realm: the arena of unceasing action. This failure testifies to the resilience of her theory of politics and to the strength of her conviction that the *vita activa* and the *vita contemplativa* represent different and distinct patterns of human life. Had she lived to write the part on Judging, she might well have recast the relationship between mind and politics, but I doubt that she would have done so. One reason is that she already felt that her rediscovery of the *vita activa* and her theory of politics owed more to the "viewpoint of the *vita contemplativa*" than she would have liked.[16] Furthermore, to recast this relationship would be to recast it necessarily in favour of the mind and against freedom, action, and indeed politics. The primacy of the mind, in the smallest measure, over the realm of politics would undermine the latter as effectively as Plato had undermined the genius and the promise of the Athenian *polis* in his *philosophical* theory of politics. Faced with this conundrum, Arendt was at a loss to specify precisely the relevance of judging, a faculty of the Mind, to politics, without circumscribing it to the point of destroying it.

But she sensed that her heroic conception of politics could not endure if it failed to muster sufficient humanity to combat irruptions of wanton violence and mass murder in the body politic. She was troubled by its moral inadequacy and she hoped and believed that the "public" faculty of judging, in which "sharing-the-world-with-others comes to pass,"[17] would bridge the chasm between thinking and acting, without endangering the realm of freedom or tacitly sanctioning all manner of evil deeds. The fact remains, however, that she did not write the crucial part on Judging.[18]

The Life of the Mind, including the remarks on Judging, advances no argument which bears on her political theory. Nor does the *Life* necessitate rethinking the sharp distinction she drew between the *vita activa* and the *vita contemplativa*. As Arendt intended it to be, the *Life* is about "transpolitical things."

NOTES

1 "Thinking and Moral Considerations," *Social Research* (Autumn 1971): 417-446, especially 438; *Life* I: 177, 179-180.

2 Ibid.

3 Hans Jonas, "Acting, Knowing, Thinking: Gleanings from Hannah Arendt's philosophical work," *Social Research* (Spring 1977): 28 (emphasis added).

4 *Life* I: 15, 22, 69-71, 177, 179-180, 212, *passim*; *OR*: 474, 502 (footnote).

5 *Life* II: 6-8, 108-110, 136, 141, 158, *passim*; *Life* I: 213.

6 "Stopping to Think," *The New York Review of Books* (October 26, 1978): 19.

7 "Hannah Arendt's Testimony," *The Massachusetts Review*, Summer 1979: 369-376.

8 "*Vita activa* and *vita contemplativa*: Reflections on Hannah Arendt's Political Thought in *The Life of the Mind*," in the *Review of Politics* (July 1981): 323-354.

9 Ibid.: 324.

10 For example, see J. Glenn Gray's essay, "The Abyss of Freedom and Hannah Arendt," in *Hannah Arendt: Recovery of the Public World*, ed. M. A. Hill (New York, 1979): 225-244.

11 *Life* I: 192; "Thinking and Moral Considerations," *op. cit.*: 446.

12 *BPF*: 219-220, *passim*.

13 *BPF*: 219-222; *Life* II: 255-272.

14 *Life* I: 192-193; *Life* II: 260-262, *passim*.

15 *Life* II: 271.

16 Arendt in *Hannah Arendt*, ed. M. A. Hill: 305.

17 *BPF*, "The Crisis in Culture:" 221; see also Michael Denneny's valiant but unsuccessful effort to uncover her theory of judging—"The Privilege of Ourselves," in *Hannah Arendt*, ed. M. A. Hill: 245-274.

18 Elisabeth Young-Bruehl's passing remark on this matter is right on the mark, in her *Hannah Arendt: For Love of the World* (New Haven, 1982): 473: "Had her 'Judging' section been written—it is tempting to say had Arendt been *able* to write 'Judging' . . .".

Selected writings
on Arendt

Abel, Lionel. "The Aesthetics of Evil: Hannah Arendt on Eichmann and the Jews," *Partisan Review* 30 (Summer 1963), 211-230.

Barnard, F. M. "Infinity and Finality: Hannah Arendt on Politics and Truth," *Canadian Journal of Social and Political Theory* 13 (September 1977), 29-57.

Bell, Daniel. "The Alphabet of Justice," *Partisan Review* 30 (Fall 1963), 417-429.

Bernauer, James. "(Mis-)reading Arendt," *Philosophy and Social Criticism* (Summer 1985), 1-34.

Bernstein, Richard J. "Hannah Arendt: The Ambiguities of Theory and Practice," in *Political Theory and Praxis*, ed. Terence Ball (Minneapolis, University of Minnesota Press, 1977).

Blanshard, Brand. "Reflections on History," *New York Times Book Review* (February 15, 1959), 26.

Bondy, François. "On Misunderstanding Eichmann," *Encounter* (November 1961), 32-37.

Botstein, Leon. "Hannah Arendt: The Jewish Question," *New Republic* (October 21, 1978), 32-37.

_____ . "Hannah Arendt," *Partisan Review* 45 (No. 3) 1978, 368-380.

Canovan, Margaret. *The Political Thought of Hannah Arendt* (London, J. M. Dent, 1974).

_____ . "The Contradictions of Hannah Arendt's Political Thought," *Political Theory* 6 (February 1978), 5-26.

Cooper, Leroy A. "Hannah Arendt's Political Philosophy: An Interpretation," *Review of Politics* 38 (April 1976), 145-176.

Dossa, Shiraz. "Hannah Arendt on Political Zionism," *Arab Studies Quarterly* 3 (Summer 1986), 219-230.

Elevitch, Bernard. "Hannah Arendt's Testimony," *Massachusetts Review* 2 (Fall 1963), 53-73.

Fruchter, Norman. "Arendt's Eichmann and Jewish Identity," in *For a New America*, ed. James Weinstein and David W. Eakins (New York, Vintage, 1970).

Gunnell, John. *Political Theory: Tradition and Interpretation* (Cambridge, Winthrop, 1979).

Heather, Gerald P. and Matthew Stolz. "Hannah Arendt and the Problem of

Critical Theory," *Journal of Politics* 41 (February 1979), 2-22.

Hill, Melvyn A., ed. *Hannah Arendt: The Recovery of the Public World* (New York, St. Martin's Press, 1979).

Hinchman, Lewis P. and Sandra K. Hinchman. "In Heidegger's Shadow: Hannah Arendt's Phenomenological Humanism," *Review of Politics* 46 (April 1984), 183-211.

Jay, Martin. "Hannah Arendt," *Partisan Review* 45 (No. 3) 1978, 248-368.

Kateb, George. *Hannah Arendt: Conscience, Politics, Evil* (Oxford, Martin Robertson, 1984).

Kazin, Alfred. *New York Jew* (New York, Vintage, 1979).

Levin, Martin. "On *Animal Laborans* and *Homo Politicus* in Hannah Arendt," *Political Theory* 4 (November 1979), 521-531.

McCarthy, Mary. *The Writing on the Wall and Other Literary Essays* (New York, Harcourt, Brace and World, 1970).

O'Sullivan, N. K. "Politics, Totalitarianism and Freedom: The Political Thought of Hannah Arendt," *Political Studies* 21 (June 1973), 183-198.

Parekh, Bhikhu. *Hannah Arendt and the Search for a New Political Philosophy* (Atlantic Highlands, Humanities Press, 1981).

Pitkin, Hanna Fenichel. "Justice: On Relating Private and Public," *Political Theory* 9 (August 1981), 327-352.

Podhoretz, Norman. *Doings and Undoings* (New York, Noonday Press, 1964).

Rosenberg, Harold. *Act and the Actor* (New York, World Publishing, 1970).

Rubenstein, Richard L. *The Cunning of History: The Holocaust and the American Future* (New York, Harper Colophon, 1978).

Shklar, Judith N. "Hannah Arendt's Triumph," *New Republic* (December 27, 1975), 8-10).

Sternberger, Dolf. "The Sunken City: Hannah Arendt's Idea of Politics," *Social Research* 44 (Spring 1977), 132-146.

Suchting, W. A. "Marx and Hannah Arendt's *The Human Condition*," *Ethics* 73 (October 1962), 47-55.

Syrkin, Marie. "Hannah Arendt: The Clothes of the Empress," *Dissent* 10 (Autumn 1963), 344-352.

Voegelin, Eric. "The Origins of Totalitarianism," *Review of Politics* 15 (January 1953), 68-76.

Vollrath, Ernst. "Hannah Arendt and the Method of Political Thinking," *Social Research* 44 (Spring 1977), 160-182.

Whitfield, Stephen J. *Into the Dark: Hannah Arendt and Totalitarianism* (Philadelphia, Temple University Press, 1980).

Wolin, Sheldon S. "Hannah Arendt and the Ordinance of Time," *Social Research* 44 (Spring 1977), 91-105.

_____ . "Stopping to Think," *New York Review of Books* (October 26, 1978), 16-21.

Yarbrough, Jean and Peter Stern. *"Vita Activa* and *Vita Contemplativa*: Reflections on Hannah Arendt's Political Thought in *The Life of the Mind,"* *Review of Politics* 43 (July 1981), 323-354.

Young-Bruehl, Elisabeth. *Hannah Arendt: For Love of the World* (New Haven, Yale University Press, 1982).

_____ . "Reflections on Hannah Arendt's *The Life of the Mind,"* *Political Theory* 10 (May 1982), 277-305.

Index